The Essential Guide to Bitcoin

The Ultimate Guide to Understanding and Investing in Bitcoin

Alex Parker

Table of Contents

INTRODUCTION

Welcome to "The Essential Guide to Bitcoin: The Ultimate Guide to Understanding and Investing in Bitcoin." We shall set out on a quest to demystify the Bitcoin world in this extensive e-book, equipping you with the information and self-assurance you need to successfully traverse this intriguing field.

Bitcoin has grabbed the attention of millions of people worldwide in recent years. Bitcoin, which was developed in 2009 by the mysterious person known only as Satoshi Nakamoto, introduced a revolutionary technology called blockchain, which completely changed how we understand and exchange money. Beyond its practical applications, Bitcoin challenges established financial systems by embodying a potent concept of decentralization, privacy, and financial sovereignty.

This e-book aims to give you a firm grasp of Bitcoin, covering everything from its origins to its current relevance in the world of international finance. This e-book will meet your needs whether you're a beginner trying to understand the fundamentals or an investor curious to learn more about Bitcoin's potential as an asset.

We'll look into the past of Bitcoin in the first few chapters, discovering how this revolutionary digital currency came to be and examining its early setbacks and achievements. Understanding the fundamental ideas that drive Bitcoin's operations, such as the innovative blockchain technology and mining processes, will help you fully realize how this peer-to-peer electronic cash system functions.

As you continue reading the e-book, you will discover helpful advice on how to buy your first Bitcoin, discover different wallet options, and put important security measures in place to safeguard your valuable digital assets. We will also examine the investment potential of Bitcoin by examining risk considerations, past price movements, and several methods for integrating Bitcoin into your investment plan.

In order to provide you a comprehensive understanding of the cryptocurrency market, we will cover not only Bitcoin but also other notable digital assets, or "altcoins," and talk about how portfolio diversification can reduce risk.

Furthermore, we will go beyond just the financial aspect of matters, looking at actual applications of Bitcoin in remittances, payment systems, and personal empowerment in developing countries.

Together, we'll explore the changing regulatory environment that surrounds Bitcoin, clarifying the tax implications and legal ramifications to make sure you stay in compliance with the law.

Lastly, we will take a look at Bitcoin's future and talk about possible developments as well as obstacles this ground-breaking cryptocurrency may face.

"The Essential Guide to Bitcoin: The Ultimate Guide to Understanding and Investing in Bitcoin" seeks to be your reliable companion in navigating the fascinating world of digital currencies, regardless of your level of computing expertise. Our mission is to provide you with the information, understanding, and tools you need to take advantage of the potential this revolutionary financial innovation presents and make wise decisions.

Together, let's take on this fascinating adventure as we uncover the mysteries of Bitcoin and embrace its potential for a decentralized, global financial future. Let the adventure begin!

CHAPTER I

Understanding Bitcoin

What is Bitcoin?

In today's rapidly evolving digital age, one term that has taken the world by storm is "Bitcoin." This revolutionary digital currency has captured the imagination of millions, challenging traditional notions of money and finance. In this section, we will delve into the depths of Bitcoin, exploring its origins, inner workings, and the transformative impact it has had on the global financial landscape.

Bitcoin, created in 2009 by an enigmatic figure known as Satoshi Nakamoto, is a decentralized digital currency. Unlike traditional fiat currencies, Bitcoin operates on a peer-to-peer network, allowing direct transactions between users without the requirement for intermediaries like banks or financial institutions. At its core lies a groundbreaking technology called blockchain, a distributed and immutable ledger that records all Bitcoin transactions securely and transparently.

The fundamental philosophy behind Bitcoin is decentralization. Traditional currencies are issued and managed by central authorities like governments and banks, but Bitcoin empowers individuals by removing the need for centralized control. Instead, the entire Bitcoin network is collectively managed by its users, making it resistant to censorship and control by any single entity. This essence of decentralization gives Bitcoin its unique character and has attracted individuals seeking financial freedom and sovereignty.

The underlying technology driving Bitcoin's operation is the blockchain. The blockchain is essentially a series of blocks, each containing a collection of transactions. Every block that is added to the chain is unchangeable and acts as a historical log of every transaction that has ever taken place on the network. This robustness ensures transparency and security, as tampering with any block would require altering all subsequent blocks, an immensely difficult task due to the computational power required.

Bitcoin transactions are processed and secured through a process known as mining. Miners are participants in the network who use powerful computers to solve complex mathematical puzzles, validating transactions and adding them to the blockchain. As an incentive, miners are rewarded with newly minted bitcoins for their efforts, thus ensuring the constant flow of new coins into circulation. Since mining prevents fraudulent transactions and double-spending, it is essential to preserving the integrity and security of the Bitcoin network.

A defining characteristic of Bitcoin is its limited supply. Satoshi Nakamoto designed Bitcoin to have a maximum supply of 21 million coins, making it inherently deflationary. The scarcity of Bitcoin is mathematically predetermined, in opposed to traditional fiat currencies, which can be issued at any time by central banks. This scarcity has fueled debates over its potential to act as a store of value, much like precious metals such as gold.

Another aspect that sets Bitcoin apart is its pseudonymity. While all transactions on the blockchain are public and transparent, users are identified by alphanumeric addresses rather than personal information. This provides a degree of privacy, as the real-world identities of users remain concealed. However, it also raises concerns about the utilization of Bitcoin for illegal activities, like tax evasion and money laundering, prompting discussions around regulation and oversight.

Bitcoin's rapid rise in popularity has led to its recognition as a viable alternative to traditional financial systems. As an investment asset, Bitcoin has exhibited remarkable price volatility, attracting both speculators seeking short-term gains and long-term investors seeking to diversify their portfolios. The exponential growth in its value over the years has been a subject of much discussion, with proponents touting it as "digital gold" and critics warning of potential bubbles and risks.

In addition to its investment potential, Bitcoin has found practical use cases in various industries. With its ability to facilitate low-cost and fast cross-border transactions, it has been hailed as a potential disruptor in the remittance market, where high fees and lengthy processing times have long been a pain point for individuals sending money to their families in other countries. Bitcoin has also been embraced by merchants as a payment method, especially in online transactions, due to its borderless and irreversible nature.

While Bitcoin's adoption and acceptance continue to grow, it has faced challenges and controversies. Scaling the network to accommodate a growing number of transactions has been a persistent concern. Solutions like the Lightning Network have been proposed to address this issue, aiming to enable faster and cheaper transactions by conducting them off-chain.

Moreover, Bitcoin's association with illicit activities on the dark web has raised questions about its ethics and societal impact. As with any disruptive technology, there are both positive and negative aspects to consider, and the ongoing dialogue on the regulation and responsible use of Bitcoin remains crucial.

In conclusion, Bitcoin is a groundbreaking innovation that has revolutionized the concept of money and finance. Born out of the vision for a decentralized and censorship-resistant currency, it has grown to become a global phenomenon, captivating individuals from all walks of life. Powered by blockchain technology and driven by the principles of decentralization, scarcity, and privacy, Bitcoin offers a glimpse into the potential future of finance.

As it continues to evolve and shape the financial landscape, Bitcoin poses both opportunities and challenges. Understanding its intricacies and implications is essential for anyone looking to participate in this digital revolution. Whether as a means of investment, a vehicle for financial empowerment, or a tool for innovative solutions, Bitcoin's impact on the world is undeniable. As we move forward into this new era of digital finance, the journey of Bitcoin remains an exciting and transformative one.

The history of Bitcoin

The story of Bitcoin is one of the most captivating narratives of the digital age, tracing its roots back to a time when the world was grappling with the aftermath of the global financial crisis. Born out of the vision of an anonymous entity known as Satoshi Nakamoto, Bitcoin emerged in 2009 as the world's first decentralized digital currency, forever altering the landscape of finance and ushering in the era of cryptocurrencies.

The whitepaper with the title of "Bitcoin: A Peer-to-Peer Electronic Cash System," authored by Satoshi Nakamoto and released in October 2008, is where Bitcoin first appeared. The article described the fundamentals of a novel digital money that would enable peer-to-peer transactions directly and without the use of middlemen. It proposed a solution to the longstanding problem of double-spending, where digital currencies could be duplicated and used fraudulently. Satoshi Nakamoto's creation was revolutionary, combining the concept of electronic cash with the principles of decentralized control and cryptographic security.

On January 3, 2009, the first-ever block on the Bitcoin blockchain, called the "genesis block" or "block zero," was mined by Nakamoto. Embedded within the block was the now-famous message: "The Times 03/Jan/2009 Chancellor on brink of second bailout for banks." This message not only marked the inception of Bitcoin but also served as a poignant commentary on the prevailing financial system's failures and the impetus behind Nakamoto's vision for a decentralized alternative.

In the early days, Bitcoin's adoption was limited to a small community of tech enthusiasts and cryptography aficionados. The initial miners and users mined and traded bitcoins on online forums and mailing lists. In May 2010, Bitcoin achieved a significant milestone when a developer named Laszlo Hanyecz made the first-ever real-world transaction using Bitcoin, purchasing two pizzas for 10,000 bitcoins. This transaction highlighted Bitcoin's potential as a means of exchange, even though its value at the time was relatively low.

As the community grew, the need for a platform to exchange bitcoins became evident. In July 2010, the first cryptocurrency exchange, "BitcoinMarket.com," was established, paving the way for a burgeoning ecosystem of trading platforms. This development further facilitated Bitcoin's adoption and led to a surge in its popularity.

Bitcoin's early years were marked by several challenges and controversies. One of the most notable events occurred in June 2011 when the largest Bitcoin exchange at the time, "Mt. Gox," suffered a major security breach, resulting in the thousands of bitcoins being stolen. This incident highlighted the importance of security in the nascent cryptocurrency space and underscored the need for robust measures to protect users' funds.

Despite the setbacks, Bitcoin's growth and development continued. In November 2012, Bitcoin underwent its first-ever halving event, reducing the block reward for miners from 50 to 25 bitcoins. This event, programmed to occur approximately every four years, further emphasized Bitcoin's deflationary nature and scarcity, as the total supply of bitcoins is capped at 21 million.

The year 2013 was a defining moment for Bitcoin as it experienced a meteoric rise in value and public attention. In April 2013, Bitcoin's price surpassed $100 for the first time, attracting widespread media coverage. As the news spread, more individuals and investors began taking an interest in this novel digital currency. Bitcoin's price continued to surge, reaching over $1,000 by the end of the year, prompting debates and discussions about its legitimacy and potential as an investment asset.

However, the price volatility that accompanied Bitcoin's ascent also attracted skepticism and criticism. Detractors labeled it a speculative bubble that would inevitably burst, drawing comparisons to historical market bubbles like the Dutch Tulip Mania. The cryptocurrency faced a period of price correction, but the fundamental technology and philosophy behind Bitcoin remained intact, continuing to attract proponents and enthusiasts.

In the subsequent years, Bitcoin's development saw increased efforts from the wider community. Developers, businesses, and organizations contributed to the improvement of the Bitcoin protocol, seeking solutions to scalability issues and exploring innovative applications of the blockchain technology.

In August 2017, Bitcoin underwent another significant milestone as it experienced its second halving, reducing the block reward to 12.5 bitcoins. This event occurred amidst a surge in public interest, with Bitcoin's price reaching an all-time high of nearly $20,000 in December 2017. The surge in price also led to a surge in transactions, causing congestion on the Bitcoin network and raising concerns about its scalability.

The year 2018 witnessed a notable market correction, with Bitcoin's price experiencing a significant decline from its peak. This downturn was part of a broader market correction that affected the entire cryptocurrency space. Despite the price volatility, the development of Bitcoin and the underlying blockchain technology continued to progress.

In the years following the market correction, Bitcoin's utility and acceptance saw gradual growth. More businesses and merchants began accepting Bitcoin as a form of payment, and financial institutions and governments started to explore the potential of blockchain technology for various use cases beyond cryptocurrencies.

As of the time of writing, Bitcoin has firmly established itself as a major player in the global financial landscape. It is recognized as a legitimate asset class by institutional investors, and the broader public has become increasingly familiar with its features and potential.

While Bitcoin's journey has been marked by remarkable growth and resilience, it has not been without its challenges. Scalability, regulatory scrutiny, and the ongoing quest for wider adoption remain areas of active development and exploration.

The story of Bitcoin continues to evolve, with ongoing debates and discussions shaping its future trajectory. As we look ahead, the world of cryptocurrencies and blockchain technology holds the potential to disrupt traditional financial systems and offer new possibilities for global financial inclusion, transparency, and efficiency.

In conclusion, the history of Bitcoin is a saga of innovation, resilience, and transformation. From its humble beginnings as an idea in a white paper to a global phenomenon, Bitcoin has defied expectations and sparked a wave of technological advancement. It has not only introduced a new form of digital currency but also ignited a revolution in finance and opened the door to an array of possibilities yet to be fully explored. The journey of Bitcoin continues to captivate the world, and as it enters its next chapter, its impact on the future of finance remains a topic of great anticipation and fascination.

How does Bitcoin work?

The world's first decentralized digital currency, Bitcoin, has captured the imagination of millions, challenging traditional notions of money and finance. At the heart of Bitcoin's revolutionary concept lies a groundbreaking technology called blockchain. In this section, we will delve into the inner workings of Bitcoin, exploring the underlying principles, the mechanics of transactions, the role of miners, and the security measures that make it a secure and transparent digital currency.

At its core, Bitcoin operates on a decentralized peer-to-peer network. Unlike traditional fiat currencies, which are issued and controlled by central authorities like governments and banks, Bitcoin relies on a distributed ledger known as the blockchain. This immutable and transparent ledger records all Bitcoin transactions, ensuring security and transparency while eliminating the need for intermediaries.

Transactions on the Bitcoin network occur between individual users who hold Bitcoin wallets. Each wallet is associated with a unique alphanumeric address, acting as a public key, and a private key known only to the owner. These keys play a crucial role in the security and authenticity of transactions.

When a user starts a Bitcoin transaction, they sign it with their private key, providing cryptographic proof of ownership and consent. This signature ensures that the transaction is valid and originated from the rightful owner. The transaction is then broadcast to the network, where it awaits validation by Bitcoin miners.

Bitcoin miners play a vital role in processing and securing transactions on the network. Mining is a process that entails solving complicated mathematical puzzles, which act as proof of work. Miners compete to find a solution for these puzzles, and the first to succeed gets to add a novel block of transactions to the blockchain.

The process of mining not only validates transactions but also creates new bitcoins. As an incentive for their efforts, miners are rewarded with a fixed amount of bitcoins for each block they successfully mine. This is the mechanism through which new bitcoins are introduced into circulation, and it is designed to mimic the process of mining precious metals like gold, thus earning the nickname "digital gold."

Bitcoin's issuance rate is set to decrease over time through a predefined schedule known as "halving." Approximately every four years, the block reward that miners receive is halved, reducing the rate of new bitcoin creation. This halving mechanism ensures a fixed maximum supply of 21 million bitcoins, making it a deflationary currency and a store of value.

The security of the Bitcoin network is a crucial aspect that ensures the integrity of transactions and the immutability of the blockchain. As the blockchain grows, the cryptographic links between blocks create a chain of transactions, making it incredibly difficult to alter any transaction history without changing all subsequent blocks. This makes the blockchain tamper-proof and transparent, as anyone can verify the entire transaction history.

Bitcoin's security is further enhanced through its consensus mechanism known as "proof of work." To alter the blockchain or execute fraudulent transactions, an attacker would need to regulate a majority of the network's computational power, which is highly impractical due to the vast network of miners distributed globally.

However, Bitcoin's reliance on proof of work has raised concerns about its environmental impact. The energy-intensive mining process consumes a significant amount of electricity, leading to debates about its sustainability and carbon footprint. In response, developers and researchers have explored alternative consensus mechanisms, like "proof of stake," to achieve consensus in a more eco-friendly manner.

To store their bitcoins securely, users utilize various types of Bitcoin wallets. These wallets come in several forms, including hardware wallets, software wallets, and paper wallets. Hardware wallets, for example, are physical devices that store private keys offline, providing robust security against online threats and hacking attempts.

While Bitcoin transactions are pseudonymous, meaning users' real-world identities are concealed behind their alphanumeric addresses, they are not entirely private. By nature, all transactions on the blockchain are open to the public and visible to everybody. Due to this, privacy-focused cryptocurrencies and solutions for Bitcoin have been developed. One such solution is the Lightning Network, which allows for more rapid and private transactions by processing them off-chain.

Bitcoin's value and utility have grown significantly over the years. Initially viewed as an experiment and a novelty, it has now garnered recognition as a legitimate asset class. As a result, numerous cryptocurrency exchanges have emerged, allowing users to buy, sell, and trade bitcoins with ease.

Bitcoin has found use cases beyond investment and speculation. Its borderless and permissionless nature has made it a viable means of remittance, facilitating international money transfers for people at a lesser cost and with quicker processing than with established financial systems.

As we move forward, Bitcoin's continued development and adoption hold the potential to transform finance on a global scale. Despite its challenges and criticisms, Bitcoin remains at the forefront of the cryptocurrency revolution, acting as a catalyst for innovative solutions and reshaping the way we perceive and transact value.

In conclusion, Bitcoin's unique architecture, driven by blockchain technology and proof of work consensus, has revolutionized the concept of money and finance. Its decentralized nature, deflationary properties, and security measures have made it a global phenomenon with significant implications for the future of finance. As the world continues to explore the potential of blockchain technology and cryptocurrencies, Bitcoin stands as a testament to the power of decentralized innovation and its ability to reshape the world's financial landscape.

Key characteristics of Bitcoin

Bitcoin, the pioneering cryptocurrency that sparked a revolution in the financial world, possesses several key characteristics that set it apart from conventional fiat currencies and other assets. As the world's first decentralized digital currency, Bitcoin operates on a groundbreaking technology called blockchain, which underpins its core principles and functionalities. In this section, we will explore the key characteristics of Bitcoin, including its decentralization, limited supply, pseudonymity, and immutability, and analyze how these features contribute to its unique value proposition and widespread appeal.

One of the most defining features of Bitcoin is its decentralized nature. Traditional fiat currencies are controlled and regulated by central authorities, such as governments and central banks. In contrast, Bitcoin runs on a peer-to-peer network, meaning it relies on a vast network of computers and users spread across the globe to process transactions and maintain the blockchain. This decentralized approach empowers individuals by eliminating the need for intermediaries, enabling users to transact directly with one another without the intervention of financial institutions or governments. Decentralization not only enhances financial freedom but also makes Bitcoin resistant to censorship and control by any single entity, ensuring greater transparency and trust in the system.

Another critical characteristic of Bitcoin is its limited supply. Satoshi Nakamoto, the unknown creator of Bitcoin, designed the digital currency with a fixed maximum supply of 21 million bitcoins. This scarcity is programmed into the system through a process called mining, where new bitcoins are issued as rewards for miners who validate transactions and secure the network. The issuance rate is halved approximately every four years through a mechanism known as "halving," ensuring a predictable and diminishing rate of new bitcoin creation. This deflationary nature of Bitcoin contrasts sharply with conventional fiat currencies, which can be printed by central authorities at will. As a result, Bitcoin's limited supply has led to comparisons with precious metals like gold, with some proponents dubbing it "digital gold."

Bitcoin transactions offer a degree of pseudonymity, providing privacy for users while maintaining transparency on the blockchain. When a user conducts a Bitcoin transaction, they are identified by an alphanumeric address, acting as a pseudonym. While these addresses do not reveal the user's real-world identity, all transactions are registered on the public blockchain and can be seen by anyone. This feature ensures transparency and immutability, allowing anyone to verify the integrity of transactions. However, it also raises concerns about the potential for blockchain analysis and the use of Bitcoin for illicit activities. To address these concerns, various privacy-focused solutions have been proposed, allowing users to enhance the confidentiality of their transactions.

Immutability is a fundamental characteristic of the Bitcoin blockchain. Once a transaction is included in a block and added to the blockchain, it becomes virtually impossible to alter or delete without the consensus of the majority of the network. This immutability is achieved through cryptographic hashing, where each block contains a unique digital fingerprint (hash) based on its contents. Any modification to a block would change its hash, requiring all subsequent blocks to be recalculated, an extremely computationally intensive task. This makes the Bitcoin blockchain highly resistant to tampering and ensures the integrity of the transaction history, which is critical for building trust in the system.

Bitcoin's design also embraces openness and transparency. The entire source code of Bitcoin is open-source, meaning it is available for anyone to view, use, and modify. This transparency fosters collaboration and innovation within the community, allowing developers to contribute to the improvement and security of the Bitcoin protocol. The open-source nature of Bitcoin has enabled the creation of various forks and alternative implementations, each catering to specific use cases or addressing specific concerns. Moreover, the public nature of the blockchain allows anyone to audit and scrutinize the network, adding an extra layer of accountability and assurance.

The decentralization and borderless nature of Bitcoin enable individuals to access and use the cryptocurrency regardless of geographical location or political affiliation. This has made Bitcoin particularly attractive in regions with insufficient access to traditional banking services or unstable financial systems. For individuals living under repressive regimes, Bitcoin offers an alternative financial infrastructure, allowing them to store and transfer value securely and discreetly. Additionally, Bitcoin has proven useful for remittances, offering a faster and cheaper substitute to traditional cross-border transactions that are often burdened with high fees and lengthy processing times.

Bitcoin's key characteristics have attracted diverse interest and applications. As an investment asset, Bitcoin has experienced significant price appreciation over the years, drawing the attention of institutional and retail investors alike. Its scarcity and deflationary nature have led some to view it as a hedge against inflation and economic uncertainties. Moreover, Bitcoin's potential as a store of value has led to comparisons with traditional safe-haven assets like gold.

Beyond investment, Bitcoin has also emerged as a means of transacting and storing wealth, particularly for those seeking to escape the limitations and risks associated with traditional banking systems. The rise of Bitcoin as a digital payment method has been facilitated by the growing acceptance of merchants worldwide, making it increasingly practical for everyday transactions.

However, Bitcoin's journey has not been without challenges. The rapid growth in popularity and adoption has at times strained the network's capacity, leading to congestion and higher transaction fees. This scalability issue has prompted debates and proposals for solutions, including the development of off-chain scaling solutions like the Lightning Network.

Moreover, the decentralized and open nature of Bitcoin has led to a diverse range of opinions and visions within the community. Disagreements over the direction of development have resulted in contentious debates and forks, leading to the creation of alternative cryptocurrencies like Bitcoin Cash and Bitcoin SV.

In conclusion, the key characteristics of Bitcoin have contributed to its extraordinary rise as a revolutionary digital currency. Its decentralization, limited supply, pseudonymity, immutability, and transparency have reshaped the way we perceive and interact with money and finance. As the world continues to explore the potential of blockchain technology and cryptocurrencies, Bitcoin remains a testament to the power of decentralized innovation and its ability to challenge and transform traditional financial systems. Whether as a store of value, a medium of exchange, or a tool for financial empowerment, Bitcoin's impact on the global financial landscape is undeniable, and its journey continues to be one of intrigue, evolution, and endless possibilities.

CHAPTER II

How to Get Bitcoin

Creating a Bitcoin wallet

In the realm of cryptocurrencies, a Bitcoin wallet is a fundamental tool for securely storing, sending, and receiving bitcoins. As the world's first decentralized digital currency, Bitcoin's unique characteristics, such as decentralization, limited supply, and pseudonymity, demand a secure and user-friendly wallet solution. In this section, we will explore the various types of Bitcoin wallets available, discuss the importance of wallet security, and provide a step-by-step guide on how to create and use a Bitcoin wallet effectively.

A Bitcoin wallet is essentially a software or hardware application that stores the user's private keys, which are vital for accessing and managing their bitcoins. These wallets interact with the Bitcoin network, enabling users to generate new addresses for receiving bitcoins, sign transactions to spend bitcoins, and view their transaction history. Bitcoin wallets come in various forms, each with its own set of features, security measures, and user interfaces to cater to the diverse needs of cryptocurrency enthusiasts.

The first decision to make when creating a Bitcoin wallet is to choose between the two broad categories: hardware wallets and software wallets. Hardware wallets are tangible devices that provide a further layer of security by storing private keys offline. They are typically small, portable devices equipped with a screen and buttons for interaction. In contrast, software wallets are applications that can be installed on computers, smartphones, or tablets, offering greater convenience but potentially with slightly lower security levels.

One of the most popular types of software wallets is the mobile wallet. These wallets, designed to run on smartphones, provide a practical solution for users who want to manage their bitcoins on the go. Mobile wallets are accessible through mobile applications available on major operating systems like the iOS and Android. They offer a user-friendly interface, making them suitable for beginners and regular bitcoin users alike. However, since mobile devices are susceptible to malware and hacking, it is crucial to choose reputable wallet providers and practice good security habits, such as keeping the device's operating system and applications up to date.

For those seeking a balance between security and convenience, desktop wallets offer an attractive option. These wallets are installed on computers and provide greater control over private keys compared to mobile wallets. Desktop wallets come in various formats, including full-node wallets, lightweight wallets, and multi-currency wallets. Full-node wallets download and store the entire Bitcoin blockchain, providing users with complete control over their transactions and enhanced privacy. On the other hand, lightweight wallets, also known as SPV wallets (Simple Payment Verification), do not require downloading the entire blockchain, making them faster to set up and use. Multi-currency wallets, as the name suggests, support multiple cryptocurrencies, allowing users to manage various digital assets within a single application.

Another category of software wallets is web wallets, also known as online wallets. Web wallets operate through web browsers and are accessible from any gadget or device with an internet connection. These wallets offer high convenience as users can access their bitcoins from anywhere, eliminating the need to download and install software. However, web wallets are considered less secure than other wallet types since the private keys are stored on third-party servers. As such, users must trust the wallet provider's security measures, making it crucial to opt for reputable and well-established services with a proven track record of security.

For users seeking the highest level of security, hardware wallets are the preferred choice. These physical devices store private keys offline, mitigating the risk of online attacks and malware. Hardware wallets are also known as cold wallets, as they do not require an internet connection for transactions. Users connect the hardware wallet to their computer or smartphone only when they need to send or receive bitcoins. This offline nature ensures that the private keys remain protected from potential online threats. Popular hardware wallet brands include Ledger and Trezor, both of which have earned the trust of the cryptocurrency community through their robust security features and ease of use.

Regardless of the type of wallet chosen, the process of creating a Bitcoin wallet typically involves a few simple steps. First, users need to select a wallet provider or manufacturer that best suits their needs. As mentioned earlier, reputable providers with strong security practices are essential to safeguarding one's digital wealth. Once the wallet is selected, users proceed with the installation process, which may involve downloading an application or connecting a hardware wallet to their device.

After installing or connecting the wallet, the user is prompted to generate a new Bitcoin address. This address is a unique alphanumeric identifier that serves as the public key, enabling others to send bitcoins to the wallet. The address is shareable and can be used for multiple transactions. It is essential to note that a new address should be generated for each transaction to enhance privacy and security.

As part of the wallet creation process, users are also required to create a backup of their wallet's recovery phrase or seed. This is a crucial step that should never be overlooked, as the recovery phrase serves as a backup for the private keys. If the device is lost, stolen, or malfunctions, the recovery phrase can be utilized to restore access to the wallet and its funds. It is essential to store the recovery phrase in a safe and secure location, away from prying eyes and potential threats.

Once the wallet has completed its set up, users can start receiving and sending bitcoins. To receive bitcoins, one needs to share their Bitcoin address with the sender, who can then initiate the transaction. After receiving bitcoins, they are stored in the wallet's address and are ready to be spent or saved.

When sending bitcoins from the wallet, users must input the recipient's Bitcoin address and specify the amount to be sent. The wallet will then prompt the user to sign the transaction with their private key to verify the authenticity of the transaction. After the transaction is signed, it is broadcast to the Bitcoin network, and miners validate and include it in a block on the blockchain. Once the transaction is verified by a sufficient number of blocks, the recipient's wallet reflects the new balance.

To maintain the security of the wallet, it is essential to keep software wallets and devices updated with the most recent firmware updates and security patches. Regularly backing up the wallet's recovery phrase and keeping it offline is crucial in the event of a device failure or loss. Additionally, enabling extra security measures, such as two-factor authentication (2FA), where available, adds an extra layer of protection to the wallet.

The security and accessibility of Bitcoin wallets have significantly improved over the years, making them more user-friendly and intuitive for both beginners and experienced users. However, it is essential for users to be vigilant and proactive in securing their wallets and protecting their digital assets from potential threats and vulnerabilities.

In conclusion, creating a Bitcoin wallet is a critical step for individuals seeking to venture into the world of cryptocurrencies and safely manage their bitcoins. The diverse range of wallet types, including hardware wallets and software wallets, offers various levels of security and convenience to suit different user preferences. Regardless of the chosen wallet, prioritizing security measures such as choosing reputable providers, securing recovery phrases, and keeping software up to date is essential for safeguarding one's digital wealth. As cryptocurrencies gain popularity and adoption, Bitcoin wallets play a central role in empowering individuals with financial freedom and control over their digital assets. By following best practices and staying informed about emerging security measures, users can confidently navigate the digital currency landscape and harness the transformative power of Bitcoin and blockchain technology.

Buying Bitcoin from exchanges

As the world's first decentralized digital currency, Bitcoin has captured the attention of investors and enthusiasts worldwide. With its unique characteristics, such as limited supply and decentralization, Bitcoin has emerged as a popular investment asset and a potential store of value. One of the most common ways to acquire Bitcoin is through cryptocurrency exchanges. In this section, we will explore the process of buying Bitcoin from exchanges, discussing the different types of exchanges, the steps involved in the purchase process, and essential considerations for a safe and successful investment journey.

Cryptocurrency exchanges are online platforms that enable the buying, selling, and trading of different digital assets, including Bitcoin. These exchanges act as intermediaries, matching buyers with sellers and providing a marketplace for users to transact. The first step in buying Bitcoin from an exchange is to select a reputable and trustworthy platform. Not all exchanges are created equal, and the cryptocurrency market has seen its share of scams and security breaches. It is essential to conduct thorough research, read user reviews, and choose a platform with a strong track record of security as well as customer support.

Once a suitable exchange is selected, the next step is to create an account. The account creation process typically involves providing an email address, generating a strong password, and verifying the account through a verification link or code sent to the email. Some exchanges may require additional Know Your Customer (KYC) procedures, where users must submit identification documents to comply with regulatory requirements. While KYC procedures may seem intrusive to some, they are an important measure for preventing fraud and ensuring compliance with anti-money laundering (or AML) regulations.

After successfully creating and verifying the account, users can proceed to deposit funds into their exchange wallet. Exchanges offer various deposit options, like bank transfers, credit/debit cards, and even alternative payment methods like PayPal or other cryptocurrencies. The deposit process may take some time, depending on the chosen method and the exchange's processing time.

Once funds are deposited, users are ready to purchase Bitcoin. The exchange provides a user-friendly interface where users can input the amount of Bitcoin they wish to buy and review the transaction details, such as the current price, fees, and total cost. Some exchanges also offer advanced trading features, such as limit orders and stop-loss orders, allowing users to execute trades based on predetermined criteria.

It is important to note that the price of Bitcoin can be highly volatile, and it can fluctuate significantly within a short period. Therefore, users must exercise caution and conduct thorough research before making a purchase. It is advisable to start with a small investment and gradually increase exposure to the asset as one becomes more familiar with the cryptocurrency market.

Once the purchase order is confirmed, the exchange will execute the trade, and the purchased Bitcoin will be credited to the user's exchange wallet. From there, users have the option to keep their Bitcoin stored on the exchange for convenience or transfer it to a personal Bitcoin wallet for enhanced security.
While keeping Bitcoin on an exchange wallet is convenient for quick trading, it comes with certain risks. Exchanges are central points of failure, and they have been subject to security breaches in the past. To mitigate the risk of losing funds due to exchange hacks or insolvency, it is highly recommended to store significant amounts of Bitcoin in a personal wallet.

A personal Bitcoin wallet offers more control and security over one's digital assets. There are several types of Bitcoin wallets, each with its unique advantages. Hardware wallets, also known as cold wallets, are physical devices that store private keys offline, making them highly secure against online threats. Software wallets, on the other hand, are applications that can be installed on computers or smartphones and offer a balance between security and convenience. Paper wallets, which involve printing the private keys on a physical piece of paper, are another option for those seeking a low-tech and secure storage solution.

Transferring Bitcoin from an exchange to a personal wallet is a straightforward process. Users simply need to create a Bitcoin address in their personal wallet and provide it to the exchange during the withdrawal process. It is essential to double-check the address to avoid any mistakes, as sending Bitcoin to the wrong address could result in the loss of funds. Additionally, some exchanges may impose withdrawal fees, so users should be aware of these costs before initiating the transfer.

The security of personal Bitcoin wallets is of utmost importance. Users must protect their private keys and recovery phrases diligently. Losing access to the private keys could lead to the irreversible loss of funds. It is advisable to keep multiple backups of recovery phrases and store them securely in separate physical locations. Moreover, users should be cautious of phishing attempts and ensure they only download wallet applications from reputable sources.

As users acquire Bitcoin and become more involved in the cryptocurrency market, they may explore other investment options beyond holding the asset in a personal wallet. Some exchanges offer the ability to trade Bitcoin for other cryptocurrencies or participate in initial coin offerings (ICOs) and token sales. However, it is essential to exercise caution and conduct thorough research before investing in alternative cryptocurrencies or participating in token sales, as the cryptocurrency market is relatively new and can be highly speculative.

Regulation and compliance are other critical factors to consider when buying Bitcoin from exchanges. The cryptocurrency industry operates in a rapidly evolving regulatory landscape, and the legality of Bitcoin varies from country to country. Users should be aware of their local regulations regarding cryptocurrency trading, taxation, and reporting requirements. Staying informed about regulatory updates and consulting with legal professionals if needed is essential for remaining compliant.

Another aspect to consider is the security measures implemented by the exchange. A reputable exchange should employ robust security protocols, such as two-factor authentication (2FA), cold storage for most of the funds, and regular security audits. Additionally, users should enable 2FA for their exchange accounts and use unique and strong passwords for their login credentials.

User support and customer service are also crucial considerations when choosing an exchange. A helpful and responsive support team can be invaluable in resolving issues and addressing concerns promptly. User reviews and feedback can provide beneficial insights into the calibre of customer support provided by an exchange.
In conclusion, buying Bitcoin from exchanges is a popular and accessible way for individuals to enter the world of cryptocurrencies and invest in the digital asset. With the diverse range of exchanges available, users have the flexibility to select a platform that aligns with their preferences in terms of security, fees, and trading options. By following the steps outlined in this guide and prioritizing security measures, users can navigate the process of buying Bitcoin safely and confidently. As the cryptocurrency market evolves, it is essential for users to stay knowledgeable, exercise caution, and make well-informed decisions to make the most of their investment journey with Bitcoin.

Bitcoin ATMs and peer-to-peer trading platforms

Bitcoin, the pioneering decentralized digital currency, has revolutionized the world of finance and challenged traditional monetary systems. As Bitcoin's popularity grows, so does the need for accessible and convenient ways to purchase and sell the digital asset. In this section, we will explore two significant avenues for acquiring and trading Bitcoin: Bitcoin ATMs and peer-to-peer (P2P) trading platforms. These innovative solutions have played a crucial role in expanding Bitcoin's adoption and enabling individuals worldwide to participate in the cryptocurrency revolution.

Bitcoin ATMs, also known as BTMs or Bitcoin kiosks, are physical machines that enable users to purchase or sell Bitcoin using cash or debit/credit cards. Similar to traditional ATMs, Bitcoin ATMs offer a user-friendly interface that guides users through the buying or selling process. As the demand for cryptocurrencies grows, Bitcoin ATMs have emerged as a convenient and accessible solution, offering an alternative to online exchanges.

One of the primary advantages of Bitcoin ATMs is their ease of use. Users do not need to have prior knowledge of cryptocurrency trading or possess a pre-existing digital wallet. The process is straightforward and typically involves scanning a QR code or entering a Bitcoin address to send the purchased bitcoins. For users buying Bitcoin with cash, the machine generates a paper wallet or a receipt containing the necessary information.

Bitcoin ATMs are strategically placed in various locations, including shopping malls, airports, convenience stores, and public areas, making them easily accessible to a broad audience. This accessibility helps bridge the gap between the traditional financial system and cryptocurrencies, as individuals who may not be familiar with online exchanges or banking applications can effortlessly access and transact with Bitcoin.

While Bitcoin ATMs offer convenience and accessibility, users should be aware of certain considerations. First, Bitcoin ATM fees can be higher than those of traditional exchanges, as the machines charge for their services and may include a premium on the Bitcoin price. Additionally, users should exercise caution when using ATMs in public areas, ensuring they are in a secure and private setting to prevent potential threats or scams.

Another essential aspect of Bitcoin ATMs is regulatory compliance. As the cryptocurrency industry operates in a rapidly evolving regulatory landscape, Bitcoin ATM operators must adhere to local laws and requirements. Depending on the jurisdiction, operators may need to implement Know Your Customer (KYC) procedures to verify users' identities and comply with anti-money laundering (AML) regulations.

In recent years, peer-to-peer (P2P) trading platforms have emerged as a popular and decentralized means of buying and selling Bitcoin. P2P platforms connect buyers and sellers directly, enabling them to trade cryptocurrencies without the need for intermediaries such as exchanges or brokers. This approach promotes privacy, accessibility, and increased control over the trading process.

P2P trading platforms function as online marketplaces, where users can post advertisements to buy or sell Bitcoin at their preferred prices and payment methods. When a trade is initiated, the platform acts as an escrow service, holding the Bitcoin until both parties fulfill their obligations. Once the payment is confirmed, the Bitcoin is released to the buyer's wallet.

One of the primary advantages of P2P trading platforms is the diverse range of payment options they offer. Users can choose from various methods, such as bank transfers, online payment systems, cash deposits, or even in-person trades. This flexibility accommodates users with different preferences and local banking systems, making it easier for individuals in various countries to participate in Bitcoin trading.

Furthermore, P2P platforms promote privacy by eliminating the need for users to share their personal information with third-party exchanges. The trading process is typically conducted under pseudonyms, using unique identifiers or usernames, preserving users' anonymity and reducing the risk of identity theft.

However, while P2P trading platforms offer privacy and convenience, users should be aware of potential risks. As with any P2P transaction, trust between parties is essential. Users should carefully review the reputation and feedback of potential trading partners to ensure a smooth and secure transaction. Additionally, users should be cautious of scams and fraud, as the decentralized nature of P2P platforms makes it challenging to mediate disputes and recover lost funds.

Regulatory compliance is also a crucial consideration for P2P trading platforms. Depending on the jurisdiction, operators and users may need to comply with local laws related to cryptocurrency trading, taxation, and AML regulations. Some P2P platforms have integrated KYC procedures to enhance security and comply with regulatory requirements, which may affect the level of anonymity and privacy users can maintain.

P2P trading platforms have been essential in advancing financial inclusion and increasing the use of Bitcoin, notwithstanding the associated risks and difficulties. P2P trading platforms provide an alternate way for people to access digital assets and participate in the global economy in areas where traditional banking services are not readily available.

While Bitcoin ATMs and P2P trading platforms have their unique advantages, they share the common goal of enabling individuals to access and participate in the cryptocurrency market more easily. These innovative solutions have contributed to the mainstream acceptance of Bitcoin and other cryptocurrencies, bringing digital assets closer to the general public and fostering financial empowerment.

As Bitcoin and cryptocurrencies continue to gain popularity, the development of Bitcoin ATMs and P2P trading platforms is likely to evolve further. Increased regulatory clarity, technological advancements, and improvements in user experience are expected to enhance the accessibility and functionality of these platforms.

As we look to the future, Bitcoin ATMs and P2P trading platforms are poised to continue their critical role in expanding the reach of cryptocurrencies and contributing to the broader adoption of blockchain technology. By providing users with accessible and convenient solutions for buying and selling Bitcoin, these platforms empower individuals to take control of their financial destinies and participate in the global digital economy. As the world embraces the possibilities of decentralized finance, Bitcoin ATMs and P2P trading platforms remain at the forefront of this transformative journey.

CHAPTER III

Bitcoin Storage and Security

Types of Bitcoin wallets

As the world embraces the digital revolution, cryptocurrencies have emerged as a new form of value and wealth. At the forefront of this financial transformation is Bitcoin, the pioneering decentralized digital currency. As users venture into the world of cryptocurrencies, one of the most critical considerations is the safe storage and regulation of their digital assets. Bitcoin wallets, which store private keys essential for accessing and transacting with bitcoins, play a central role in ensuring the security of users' holdings. In this section, we will explore the various types of Bitcoin wallets available, each with its unique features and security considerations, empowering individuals to make informed choices in safeguarding their digital wealth.

Software wallets, or digital wallets, are applications that run on computers, smartphones, tablets, or other electronic devices. They offer a user-friendly interface for generating and managing Bitcoin addresses, as well as sending and receiving bitcoins. Software wallets can be further classified into several subtypes, each catering to different user preferences and security levels.

Desktop wallets are installed and run on personal computers. They provide a balance between security and convenience, as they enable users to maintain control over their private keys. Desktop wallets come in various forms, including full-node wallets and lightweight wallets. Full-node wallets download and store the entire Bitcoin blockchain, offering users complete control over their transactions and enhancing privacy. On the other hand, lightweight wallets, also known as SPV (Simple Payment Verification) wallets, do not require downloading the entire blockchain, making them faster to set up and use.

Mobile wallets are designed to run on smartphones and tablets, making them a popular choice for users who want to manage their bitcoins on the go. Mobile wallets provide a user-friendly and intuitive interface, making them suitable for beginners and regular bitcoin users alike. However, users should be cautious about the security of their devices, as smartphones can be susceptible to malware and hacking attempts.

Web wallets, also known as online wallets, operate through web browsers and are accessible from any device with an internet connection. These wallets offer convenience, as users can access their bitcoins from anywhere without the need to download and install software. However, web wallets store private keys on third-party servers, making them less secure than other wallet types. Users should choose reputable and well-established web wallet providers with strong security measures to safeguard their funds.

Hardware wallets, also known as cold wallets, are physical devices designed to store private keys offline. They offer a high level of security against online threats, making them an excellent choice for users holding significant amounts of Bitcoin. Hardware wallets come in the form of small, portable devices with a screen and buttons for interaction. When connected to a computer or smartphone, they allow users to initiate and sign transactions securely. As private keys are stored offline on the hardware wallet, they are not exposed to potential online attacks.

Paper wallets are a straightforward and low-tech method of storing bitcoins securely. They involve generating and printing the private keys and corresponding Bitcoin addresses on a physical piece of paper. Paper wallets are typically created offline for enhanced security and are considered one of the most secure methods for long-term storage of bitcoins. However, users should take extra precautions to protect the paper wallet from physical damage, loss, or theft.

Brain wallets are a unique type of Bitcoin wallet that relies on users' memory to store their private keys. Users generate private keys based on a passphrase or a sequence of words they can remember. While brain wallets offer convenience and a form of "password recovery" through memory, they are inherently risky. If the passphrase is weak or easily guessable, it becomes susceptible to brute-force attacks.

Multisignature wallets, often referred to as multisig wallets, require multiple private keys to authorize transactions. For example, a 2-of-3 multisig wallet demands two out of three private keys to sign a transaction for it to be valid. Multisig wallets add an extra layer of security, as multiple parties must cooperate to initiate transactions. This makes them suitable for joint accounts, shared funds, or businesses looking for enhanced security measures.

When choosing a Bitcoin wallet, users must consider their specific needs, security requirements, and level of technical expertise. Each wallet type comes with its advantages and drawbacks, and users should weigh these factors to make an informed decision.

Security is a major concern when it comes to Bitcoin wallets. Private keys are the gateway to accessing and spending bitcoins, and losing control of them can result in irreversible loss of funds. Therefore, users must prioritize security measures, such as enabling two-factor authentication (2FA), using strong and unique passwords, and keeping software and devices updated.

Users should also be cautious of potential phishing attempts and scams that target cryptocurrency holders. Ensuring that wallet applications are downloaded from official and reputable sources and verifying the authenticity of websites before entering sensitive information is essential for protecting against phishing attacks.

Another crucial consideration is the backup of private keys or recovery phrases. Users should maintain multiple backups of their private keys or recovery phrases and store them securely in separate physical locations. This precaution guards against the loss of access to funds in the event of device failure or loss.

Regulatory compliance is also a consideration for certain wallet types. For example, exchanges and some online wallet providers may require users to undergo Know Your Customer (KYC) procedures to comply with anti-money laundering (AML) regulations. Users should be aware of the regulatory requirements in their jurisdiction and select wallet providers that align with their preferences regarding privacy and compliance.

In conclusion, Bitcoin wallets are an indispensable tool for securely storing and managing digital assets. The diverse range of wallet types, including software wallets, hardware wallets, paper wallets, brain wallets, and multisignature wallets, cater to various user preferences and security needs. As users venture into the world of cryptocurrencies, choosing the right wallet is a crucial step towards safeguarding their digital wealth. By prioritizing security measures, exercising caution, and staying informed about best practices, users can confidently navigate the cryptocurrency landscape and embark on a secure and rewarding journey with Bitcoin.

Best practices for securing your Bitcoin

As the world embraces the digital revolution, cryptocurrencies like Bitcoin have emerged as a revolutionary form of value and wealth. As users venture into the world of cryptocurrencies, securing their digital assets becomes paramount. Unlike traditional financial systems, Bitcoin operates on a decentralized and pseudonymous network, requiring users to take a proactive approach to protect their funds from potential threats and vulnerabilities. In this section, we will explore best practices for securing your Bitcoin, including the importance of private key management, the use of hardware wallets, securing online accounts, and maintaining a vigilant stance against potential scams and phishing attempts.

At the heart of Bitcoin security is the concept of private keys. Private keys are long strings of randomly generated characters that grant access to the bitcoins stored in a particular wallet address. Ensuring the utmost security of private keys is essential to safeguarding one's digital assets. When creating a Bitcoin wallet, users are provided with a recovery phrase or mnemonic seed. This recovery phrase is a sequence of words that can be used to regenerate the private keys associated with the wallet. Users must keep this recovery phrase safe and secure, as losing it could lead to the irreversible loss of funds. It is crucial to keep the recovery phrase offline in a secure location, away from prying eyes and potential threats.

Hardware wallets, also known as cold wallets, are physical devices designed specifically for the secure storage of private keys offline. These wallets provide an additional layer of protection against online threats and malware. When using a hardware wallet, private keys never leave the device and are not exposed to potential online attacks. Hardware wallets are recognized as one of the most secure methods of storing Bitcoin for long-term holdings or significant amounts. Popular hardware wallet brands include Ledger and Trezor, both known for their robust security features and ease of use.

Enabling two-factor authentication (2FA) is a simple yet effective security measure to protect online accounts, including cryptocurrency exchanges and wallets. 2FA necessitates users to provide an additional verification code, typically sent to their mobile device, along with their password when logging in or initiating transactions. This further layer of security significantly reduces the risk of illegal access to accounts, even if the password is compromised.

Securing online accounts is of utmost importance in the cryptocurrency space. Many users utilize exchanges and online wallets to buy, sell, and manage their Bitcoin. It is crucial to choose reputable and well-established platforms with a robust track record of security. Always validate the authenticity of websites before entering sensitive information, and be cautious of phishing attempts and scams. Ensure that websites have SSL (Secure Sockets Layer) encryption to protect data transmitted between the user and the website.

Phishing scams are common in the cryptocurrency world, where malicious actors attempt to deceive users into revealing their login credentials or private keys. Phishing attempts can come in the form of fake websites, emails, or messages that mimic legitimate platforms. It is essential to exercise caution and never click on doubtful links or download files from unknown sources. Always access cryptocurrency platforms directly through official websites and never share sensitive information, such as recovery phrases or private keys, with anyone.

Keeping software, operating systems, and wallet applications up to date is critical for maintaining the highest level of security. Developers regularly release updates to solve security vulnerabilities and enhance the overall performance of their software. By updating software promptly, users ensure that their wallets and devices are equipped with the latest security patches.

Creating strong and unique passwords for online accounts and wallets is a fundamental security practice. A robust password should be a combination of a uppercase and lowercase letters, numbers, and special characters. Avoid using easily guessable passwords or common phrases. Users can also employ password managers to generate and securely store their passwords.

While securing Bitcoin is essential, diversifying one's investments and managing risk is also a critical aspect of financial security. Instead of keeping all bitcoins in a single wallet or exchange, consider distributing them across multiple wallets, hardware wallets, or even offline storage solutions like paper wallets. This strategy reduces the risk of losing all funds in case of a security breach or wallet failure.

Staying informed and educated about the latest security threats and best practices is vital for protecting your Bitcoin. Joining cryptocurrency communities, participating in forums, and reading reputable sources can provide valuable insights and security tips. Education empowers users to make informed decisions and avoid falling victim to potential scams or fraudulent schemes.

Multisignature (multisig) wallets offer an extra layer of security by requiring multiple private keys to authorize transactions. For example, a 2-of-3 multisig wallet demands two out of three private keys to sign a transaction for it to be valid. Multisig wallets are especially useful for joint accounts, shared funds, or businesses seeking enhanced security measures.

In conclusion, securing Bitcoin and other cryptocurrencies is a shared responsibility between users and the broader cryptocurrency community. By implementing best practices such as private key management, using hardware wallets, enabling 2FA, securing online accounts, and staying vigilant against phishing attempts, users can significantly mitigate the risk of losing their digital assets. As the cryptocurrency landscape continues to evolve, security measures must adapt to new challenges and threats. By staying informed, prioritizing security, and employing sound risk management strategies, individuals can confidently embrace the transformative power of cryptocurrencies and safeguard their financial future in the digital age.

CHAPTER IV

Investing in Bitcoin

Evaluating the investment potential of Bitcoin

Since its birth in 2009, Bitcoin has captivated the world's attention as the first decentralized digital currency. Its revolutionary blockchain technology, limited supply, and potential to disrupt traditional financial systems have made it a popular choice among investors and enthusiasts. However, evaluating the investment potential of Bitcoin requires a comprehensive analysis of various factors. In this section, we will delve into the key aspects that investors should consider when assessing Bitcoin as an investment opportunity, including its historical performance, market trends, technological advancements, regulatory landscape, and potential risks.

One of the primary aspects to consider when evaluating Bitcoin's investment potential is its historical performance. Bitcoin has demonstrated extraordinary price volatility since its inception, with both rapid surges and steep corrections. Over the years, it has experienced significant bull and bear markets. Understanding Bitcoin's price history can provide insights into its potential future performance. Investors should analyze the historical price trends, market cycles, and the factors that have influenced Bitcoin's price movements. Additionally, considering the macro-economic events during various market cycles can help investors gauge Bitcoin's potential as a hedge against economic uncertainties.

The widespread adoption of Bitcoin is a crucial factor to assess its investment potential. The growing acceptance of cryptocurrencies by individuals, businesses, and institutions can drive increased demand and positively impact its value. Examining market trends, such as the number of Bitcoin users, merchant adoption, and institutional interest, can offer valuable insights into its long-term viability as an investment asset. Furthermore, monitoring the growth of the decentralized finance (DeFi) ecosystem, which relies heavily on blockchain technology and smart contracts, can indicate the overall health of the cryptocurrency market.

The technological advancements and innovations within the Bitcoin ecosystem are essential considerations for evaluating its investment potential. Bitcoin's underlying blockchain technology has evolved over the years, leading to improvements in scalability, security, and transaction speed. Investors should stay informed about the development and implementation of new technologies, such as the Lightning Network, Segregated Witness (SegWit), and other upgrades that can enhance Bitcoin's utility and value. Moreover, understanding the competitive landscape and the potential of emerging blockchain projects can help investors gauge Bitcoin's position as a leading cryptocurrency in the long run.

The regulatory environment is significant in shaping the investment potential of Bitcoin. Different countries have adopted varying approaches to regulate cryptocurrencies, ranging from supportive to restrictive. Regulatory developments can impact Bitcoin's liquidity, accessibility, and acceptance as a legitimate investment asset. Investors should closely monitor regulatory updates and be aware of the possible risks and opportunities that may arise due to changes in the regulatory landscape. For instance, clear and favorable regulations can provide a more secure investment environment, while regulatory uncertainty can cause temporary market fluctuations.

Like any investment, Bitcoin carries its share of risks that investors should carefully assess. The price volatility of Bitcoin can result in substantial gains, but it also exposes investors to significant losses. Investors should be prepared to withstand market fluctuations and should not invest more than they can afford to lose. Additionally, security risks, such as hacking attempts and exchange breaches, can threaten the safety of Bitcoin holdings. Employing robust security measures, such as using hardware wallets and enabling two-factor authentication, can mitigate these risks. Furthermore, staying cautious of potential scams and fraudulent schemes prevalent in the cryptocurrency space is crucial.

Diversification is a fundamental strategy to manage risk in an investment portfolio. Investors should consider Bitcoin as one component of a diversified portfolio, alongside traditional assets such as stocks, bonds, and real estate. Allocating a portion of the portfolio to Bitcoin can potentially provide diversification benefits and act as a hedge against inflation and economic uncertainty. However, the proportion of Bitcoin in a portfolio should be carefully balanced based on the investor's risk tolerance, investment goals, and time horizon.

Evaluating Bitcoin's investment potential requires a long-term perspective. Investors should conduct fundamental analysis, assessing the technology's long-term prospects and adoption trends. Analyzing Bitcoin's utility as a medium of exchange, store of value, and potential for disrupting financial systems can provide valuable insights into its investment attractiveness. Considering the supply dynamics, such as Bitcoin's fixed supply cap of 21 million coins, can also influence its long-term price trajectory. Moreover, analyzing the strength of the Bitcoin community and the active development of the protocol can indicate the coin's resilience in the face of market challenges.

The cryptocurrency market is heavily impacted by market sentiment and media coverage. News events, social media discussions, and public perception can impact Bitcoin's price movements. While market sentiment can be fickle, investors should remain objective and avoid making investment decisions based solely on short-term emotions or hype. Conducting thorough research and relying on sound analysis rather than succumbing to market noise can lead to more informed investment decisions.

Evaluating the investment potential of Bitcoin requires a comprehensive analysis of historical performance, market trends, technological advancements, regulatory landscape, risk factors, and macro-economic influences. Investors should approach Bitcoin as a long-term investment opportunity, considering its potential as a store of value and a disruptive force in the financial industry. While Bitcoin's price volatility poses risks, its limited supply and growing adoption present opportunities for those willing to navigate the cryptocurrency market responsibly. By conducting due diligence, diversifying their portfolios, and staying informed about market trends, investors can make sound decisions and potentially benefit from the investment potential of Bitcoin in the evolving digital economy. As the cryptocurrency landscape continues to mature, Bitcoin's role as a transformative financial asset is likely to endure, making it a compelling investment option for those seeking exposure to this exciting and dynamic market.

Understanding Bitcoin's price volatility

Bitcoin, as the pioneer of cryptocurrencies, has garnered significant attention and investment interest since its inception in 2009. While its potential to revolutionize finance and disrupt traditional systems has driven its popularity, Bitcoin's price volatility has been a defining characteristic of its market behavior. In this section, we will explore the factors contributing to Bitcoin's price volatility, analyze its historical price movements, and examine the implications of such volatility on investors and the broader cryptocurrency ecosystem. Understanding Bitcoin's price volatility is crucial for investors and enthusiasts alike as they navigate this dynamic and emerging digital asset.

As a relatively young and nascent asset class, the cryptocurrency market, including Bitcoin, is inherently susceptible to higher levels of price volatility compared to established financial markets. The lack of long-term price history and limited historical data make it challenging to predict price movements accurately. Additionally, the relatively smaller market capitalization of cryptocurrencies compared to traditional assets means that even small fluctuations in demand or supply can have significant impacts on prices. The evolving regulatory landscape and shifting market sentiment also contribute to the price volatility in emerging markets like cryptocurrencies.

Bitcoin's fixed supply cap of 21 million coins is a fundamental factor influencing its price volatility. As demand for Bitcoin fluctuates, its limited supply can lead to rapid price movements. When demand exceeds supply, as seen during bullish market periods, the price of Bitcoin tends to surge. Conversely, when demand recedes, and selling pressure intensifies, bearish trends can cause sharp price declines. The interchange between supply and demand in the market can be influenced by macro-economic events, investor sentiment, regulatory developments, and technological advancements.

The sentiment of market participants plays a significant role in driving Bitcoin's price volatility. Positive news and favorable developments in the cryptocurrency space can lead to surges in demand and subsequent price increases.

Similarly, negative news, regulatory uncertainties, or security breaches can trigger panic selling and sharp price declines. Additionally, speculative trading practices, such as short-term trading and leverage, amplify the impact of market sentiment on price movements. The herd mentality and emotional reactions of investors can create price bubbles and speculative manias, leading to extreme volatility.

The relatively low liquidity in the cryptocurrency market can exacerbate Bitcoin's price volatility. In smaller markets, large buy or sell orders can have outsized effects on prices. This illiquidity can make the market vulnerable to price manipulation by whales and large institutional investors. Coordinated actions to pump or dump the price, known as "pump-and-dump" schemes, can lead to sudden and drastic price swings. The prevalence of unregulated and unmonitored exchanges can further compound the risk of price manipulation.

Bitcoin's underlying technology and development updates can influence its price volatility. Improvements in the scalability, security, and utility of the Bitcoin network can bolster investor confidence and drive demand. Conversely, protocol upgrades or potential vulnerabilities can spark uncertainty and cause price fluctuations. Additionally, forks and divergences in the Bitcoin blockchain, like the Bitcoin Cash and Bitcoin SV forks, have led to market turbulence as investors navigate the implications of these splits.

As the cryptocurrency market matures, the entry of institutional investors and traditional financial institutions has begun to influence Bitcoin's price volatility. Institutional interest and adoption can stabilize prices, reduce speculative activity, and increase market liquidity. However, the involvement of institutional investors can also introduce higher levels of price correlation with traditional assets during times of global economic uncertainty.

The regulatory environment is a significant external factor impacting Bitcoin's price volatility. Changes in regulations, either supportive or restrictive, can influence investor sentiment and confidence in the cryptocurrency market. Clarity and favorable regulations can attract institutional investment and encourage market participation, leading to reduced volatility. Conversely, unclear or unfavorable regulations can lead to uncertainty, capital flight, and increased volatility. Bitcoin's

price volatility presents both opportunities and risks for investors. While periods of rapid price appreciation can yield significant returns, they are accompanied by equally substantial risks of price declines. Before investing money in Bitcoin, investors should carefully consider their financial goals and risk tolerance. Additionally, the potential for short-term gains may attract speculative traders, but it can also lead to significant losses if not managed responsibly.

Bitcoin's price volatility highlights the importance of diversification in investment portfolios. Including Bitcoin in a diversified portfolio of assets can potentially offer benefits, such as a hedge against inflation, uncorrelated returns to traditional assets, and exposure to a rapidly evolving market. However, investors should be cautious not to overweight their portfolios with Bitcoin or other cryptocurrencies, as excessive exposure can magnify risk. Investor sentiment plays a critical role in Bitcoin's price volatility. Extreme market movements driven by fear or euphoria can lead to herding behavior, where investors follow the crowd without conducting thorough analysis. Understanding the psychological aspects of market sentiment can help investors make informed decisions and avoid reacting impulsively to short-term price fluctuations.

Given Bitcoin's historical price volatility, adopting a long-term investment perspective is often recommended. Short-term price movements may be driven by speculation, but the long-term value proposition of Bitcoin lies in its potential as a store of value and a transformative technology. Investors should focus on the underlying fundamentals, technological advancements, and adoption trends rather than solely reacting to daily price swings.

Regulatory developments and legal uncertainties can significantly impact Bitcoin's price volatility. Clarity in regulations and a supportive legal framework can provide a more stable investment environment. Conversely, sudden changes in regulations or adverse legal developments can introduce uncertainty and cause short-term price turbulence.

Bitcoin's price volatility is a defining characteristic of the cryptocurrency market. Understanding the factors contributing to this volatility, such as supply and demand dynamics, market sentiment, technological advancements, regulatory developments, and market maturity, is essential for investors looking to participate in this emerging asset class. Bitcoin's price volatility offers opportunities for significant returns but also exposes investors to substantial risks. Adopting a long-term investment perspective, diversifying portfolios, and staying informed about market developments are crucial strategies for navigating Bitcoin's dynamic and evolving price landscape. As the cryptocurrency ecosystem continues to mature and regulatory clarity improves, Bitcoin's price volatility may gradually stabilize, making it a more predictable and viable investment choice for a wider range of investors.

Long-term vs. short-term investment approaches

Bitcoin, the pioneering cryptocurrency, has garnered significant attention as an investment vehicle over the years. As the cryptocurrency market develops and matures, investors are faced with a crucial decision: adopting a long-term or short-term investment approach. The long-term approach involves holding onto Bitcoin for extended periods, expecting its value to appreciate significantly over time. On the other hand, the short-term approach entails actively buying and selling Bitcoin to capitalize on short-term price movements and market trends. Both strategies offer unique advantages and challenges, and investors must carefully consider their financial goals, risk tolerance, and market expertise when choosing their investment approach in the volatile and ever-changing world of Bitcoin.

The long-term investment approach in Bitcoin is characterized by patient and enduring investment horizons, often spanning years or even decades. Long-term investors view Bitcoin as a transformative technology and a potential hedge against traditional financial systems and economic uncertainties. They believe in its potential to revolutionize finance, act as a store of value, and potentially become a globally adopted digital asset. Advocates of the long-term approach see Bitcoin as an opportunity to diversify their portfolios and participate in the ongoing digital revolution.

One of the primary advantages of the long-term approach is the potential for substantial returns over time. Bitcoin's historical price performance demonstrates periods of remarkable growth followed by corrective phases. By maintaining a long-term perspective, investors can benefit from holding through these volatile price swings and capitalize on the overall upward trajectory of Bitcoin's value. This approach reduces the impact of short-term market fluctuations and allows investors to stay focused on the broader trend of Bitcoin's growth.

Moreover, long-term investors are not burdened by the need to constantly monitor the market or make frequent trading decisions. By adopting a "buy and hold" strategy, long-term investors can avoid the stress and emotional decision-making often associated with short-term trading. Additionally, long-term investors save on transaction costs and taxes, as they are not actively buying and selling their holdings, thus preserving more of their potential returns.

However, the long-term investment approach also comes with its set of risks and considerations. The cryptocurrency market is well recognized for its high volatility, and the value of Bitcoin can experience significant fluctuations over relatively short periods. Long-term investors must possess the financial capacity to withstand these price swings and have the resilience to hold onto their investments even during bearish market conditions. The long-term nature of this strategy means that investors must be patient and not be swayed by short-term market sentiment or noise.

Furthermore, the regulatory landscape surrounding cryptocurrencies is still evolving, and governmental actions or regulations could impact the market and potentially influence long-term investment strategies. Additionally, technological advancements and competition from other cryptocurrencies could affect Bitcoin's long-term value proposition.

The short-term investment approach in Bitcoin involves actively buying and selling the cryptocurrency within relatively brief periods, ranging from days to weeks or months. Short-term investors, also known as traders, aim to profit from short-term price movements and market trends. They employ various trading strategies, such as day trading, swing trading, and momentum trading, to capitalize on short-term price volatility.

One of the primary advantages of the short-term approach is the potential for quick profits. By taking advantage of short-term price swings, traders can generate returns in a shorter timeframe compared to long-term investors. This strategy is appealing to individuals who possess expertise in technical analysis, market trends, and trading strategies, and are comfortable with taking on higher risks for potentially higher rewards.

Short-term trading enables investors to take advantage of both upward and downward price movements. In bullish market conditions, traders can buy low and sell high, seeking to maximize their gains. Conversely, in bearish conditions, they can short sell Bitcoin, which involves borrowing the cryptocurrency to sell at the current price and repurchasing it at a lower price to return the borrowed coins, thus profiting from the price decline. However, the short-term investment approach comes with its own set of challenges and risks. Timing the market accurately is notoriously difficult, and even experienced traders can make wrong predictions, leading to losses. The short-term nature of this strategy also exposes traders to higher transaction costs, as frequent buying and selling can accrue considerable fees. Additionally, the constant trading activity may lead to potential tax implications, as each trade could trigger taxable events.

The psychological aspect of short-term trading can be demanding, as traders may face stress, anxiety, and emotional decision-making in response to price fluctuations. The highly volatile characteristic of the cryptocurrency market can lead to significant losses if the right risk management is not in place. Traders must be disciplined and have a well-thought-out strategy to navigate the rapid changes in the market.

When deciding between a long-term and short-term investment approach in Bitcoin, investors should consider various factors that meet their financial goals, risk tolerance, market knowledge, and time horizon.

Long-term investing is generally considered less risky than short-term trading, as it relies on the overall growth potential of Bitcoin over time rather than short-term price movements. Investors with a higher risk tolerance and experience in market analysis may be more inclined to pursue short-term trading for potential quick profits.

Long-term investing requires a more extended time horizon, whereas short-term trading involves frequent monitoring and active decision-making. Investors should evaluate their willingness and ability to hold onto their Bitcoin holdings for extended periods or actively trade in the short term.
Successful short-term trading often requires a deep understanding of technical analysis, market trends, and trading strategies. Investors should assess their level of expertise and willingness to invest time in learning and improving their trading skills.

Short-term trading involves frequent buying and selling, leading to higher transaction costs and probable tax implications. Investors should consider the impact of these costs on their overall investment returns.
The highly volatile characteristic of the cryptocurrency market can lead to substantial price swings. Long-term investors should be prepared to withstand these fluctuations, while short-term traders should be adept at managing risks in a rapidly changing market.

Regardless of the investment approach chosen, diversification is essential to mitigate risk. Investors can diversify their portfolios by keeping a mix of assets, including Bitcoin and other cryptocurrencies, stocks, bonds, and real estate.

In the world of Bitcoin investing, the long-term and short-term approaches offer distinct opportunities and challenges. Long-term investing allows investors to capitalize on Bitcoin's potential for long-term growth and act as a store of value, while short-term trading presents the potential for quick profits from price swings. Investors should carefully take into account their financial goals, risk tolerance, market knowledge, and time horizon when choosing their investment approach.

Regardless of the chosen strategy, a prudent and informed approach to Bitcoin investing is essential. The cryptocurrency market is dynamic and constantly evolving, and investors should stay updated on market trends, regulatory developments, and technological advancements. Whether they opt for long-term or short-term investing, patience, discipline, and risk management will be crucial in navigating the volatile and promising landscape of Bitcoin investment. By considering their individual circumstances and aligning their investment approach with their financial objectives, investors can position themselves to make sound decisions and seize the opportunities offered by the ever-changing world of Bitcoin.

Recognizing Bitcoin investment scams and risks

The world of cryptocurrencies has captured the imagination of investors and enthusiasts alike, with Bitcoin leading the charge as the pioneer and most well- known digital asset. While the potential for substantial profits and the promise of a decentralized financial future have driven interest in Bitcoin and other cryptocurrencies, it has also attracted malicious actors aiming to take advantage of unsuspecting investors. In this section, we will delve into the various Bitcoin investment scams and risks that investors must be aware of to safeguard their hard-earned money and make informed decisions in the cryptocurrency market.

Ponzi schemes and pyramid schemes are among the most notorious types of investment scams that have plagued the cryptocurrency space. In a Ponzi scheme, the fraudster promises high and consistent returns on investments, but instead of generating profits through legitimate means, they use funds from latest investors to pay returns to earlier ones. This creates a cycle where investors believe they are making profits, but in reality, they are receiving their own money or that of others. Pyramid schemes operate similarly, but participants are incentivized to recruit new investors, who in turn recruit others, creating a hierarchical structure. As the scheme grows, it becomes more and more difficult to sustain, and eventually, it collapses, leaving the majority of participants with significant financial losses.

Initial Coin Offerings (ICOs) have become a popular fundraising method for new cryptocurrencies and blockchain projects. While legitimate ICOs provide an opportunity for investors to support innovative projects and potentially profit from the growth of new tokens, fake ICOs have become a breeding ground for scams. Scammers create fictitious projects with elaborate marketing campaigns, promising revolutionary technology and high returns. Unsuspecting investors, eager to participate in the next big thing, invest their money in these fake ICOs, only to find that the project does not exist, and their funds are lost forever. Conducting thorough research and due diligence before participating in any ICO is essential to identify legitimate projects and avoid falling victim to scams.

A common technique employed by scammers to steal sensitive information from unsuspecting individuals is known as phishing scams. In the cryptocurrency space, phishing attacks often target users' private keys, login credentials, or other valuable data. Scammers create fake websites that mimic legitimate cryptocurrency exchanges, wallets, or ICO platforms, tricking users into entering their private information. These scam websites are often designed to look identical to the real ones, making it difficult for users to differentiate between the two. It is crucial for investors to verify the website's URL, ensure that the site is secure (indicated by "https" in the URL), and never share their private keys or passwords with anyone.

Malicious software, such as malware and ransomware, poses a significant risk to cryptocurrency investors. Scammers use various methods to infect users' devices with malware, such as sending infected links or attachments through email or social media. Once the malware gains access to the user's computer or smartphone, it can steal cryptocurrency wallet data or even hold the user's data hostage until a ransom is paid. Ransomware attacks have become particularly prevalent in recent years, with scammers demanding payment in Bitcoin or other cryptocurrencies to unlock the user's data. Employing robust cybersecurity measures, such as using reputable antivirus software and hardware wallets for secure storage of digital assets, can help mitigate the risk of falling victim to malware and ransomware attacks.

Social media platforms have become a breeding ground for cryptocurrency scams, with scammers using various tactics to target unsuspecting users. One common social media scam involves impersonating well-known figures, celebrities, or influential individuals and using their profiles to promote fraudulent giveaways or investment opportunities. Scammers may claim that the influential figure is giving away Bitcoin or other cryptocurrencies and ask users to send a small amount of cryptocurrency to receive a more substantial reward. However, once users send their funds, the promised rewards never materialize, and they lose their money. Investors should exercise caution and refrain from participating in such giveaways or investment offers, as legitimate entities rarely request cryptocurrency transfers in this manner.

The cryptocurrency market has seen the rise of numerous exchanges, but not all of them are reputable or regulated. Unregulated exchanges may lack the necessary security measures and customer protections, leaving investors vulnerable to potential hacks or fraudulent activities. Scammers have been known to operate fake exchanges, enticing users with attractive trading offers and then disappearing with their funds. To protect themselves, investors should only use well-established and regulated exchanges that prioritize security and adhere to robust compliance standards.

Pump-and-dump schemes are another form of manipulation that poses a significant threat to investors in the cryptocurrency market. In these schemes, coordinated groups of investors artificially inflate the price of a low-cap cryptocurrency by buying large quantities, creating a buying frenzy among retail investors. As the price rises, the schemers sell their holdings at a profit, causing the price to plummet and leaving unsuspecting retail investors with significant losses. Identifying pump-and-dump schemes can be challenging, as they often involve coordinated efforts across various platforms and social media channels. Investors should exercise caution when trading low-cap cryptocurrencies with volatile price movements and avoid participating in pump-and-dump schemes.

The decentralized nature of cryptocurrencies and the lack of regulatory oversight in some jurisdictions make investors susceptible to risks and scams. Unlike traditional financial markets, cryptocurrency markets operate with minimal regulations, leaving investors with limited recourse in case of fraud or misconduct. The absence of investor protections, such as deposit insurance or recourse through regulatory authorities, exposes investors to potential losses. As a result, it is crucial for investors to be aware of this lack of protection and exercise due diligence before engaging in cryptocurrency investments.

Bitcoin's inherent price volatility is a defining characteristic of the cryptocurrency market, presenting both opportunities and risks for investors. While price volatility can lead to significant profits, it also exposes investors to heightened market risks. The price of Bitcoin can fluctuate dramatically in short periods, influenced by various factors, including market sentiment, regulatory developments, macroeconomic events, and technological advancements. Investors must be prepared for the potential for substantial price swings and only invest what they can afford to lose.

One of the significant risks faced by investors in the cryptocurrency market is the lack of understanding and education about cryptocurrencies and the underlying technology. Investing in a complex and rapidly evolving market without sufficient knowledge can lead to poor decision-making and potential losses. Many scams target inexperienced investors who may be lured by promises of quick profits without understanding the risks involved. It is essential for investors to educate themselves about cryptocurrencies, blockchain technology, and the risks associated with investing in the market. Seeking out reliable educational resources, attending webinars, or participating in online communities can help investors gain a better understanding of the cryptocurrency market and make informed decisions.

As the popularity of Bitcoin and cryptocurrencies soar, so does the prevalence of investment scams and risks. Recognizing the various types of scams, such as Ponzi schemes, fake ICOs, phishing attacks, and pump-and-dump schemes, is crucial for investors to protect themselves from financial losses. Staying informed, conducting thorough research, and exercising caution when engaging in cryptocurrency investments can help investors navigate the intricate and ever-changing landscape of digital assets. Moreover, seeking reputable exchanges, employing robust cybersecurity measures, and understanding the risks associated with market volatility are essential steps for making informed decisions in the cryptocurrency market.

As the cryptocurrency space evolves, investors must remain vigilant, informed, and discerning to navigate the risks and opportunities that come with investing in Bitcoin and other digital assets. By recognizing and understanding the various investment scams and risks, investors can position themselves to make informed decisions and seize the potential benefits offered by the transformative world of cryptocurrencies. Education, due diligence, and a cautious approach will be vital in ensuring that the cryptocurrency market remains a place of innovation and opportunity, rather than a playground for fraudsters and scammers.

CHAPTER V

Bitcoin Mining and Rewards

Mining basics and how it contributes to the network

Mining is an essential and intricate process that underpins the functionality, security, and decentralization of Bitcoin and other cryptocurrencies. It serves as the backbone of the blockchain network by validating transactions, adding new blocks to the chain, and ensuring the integrity of the entire system. In this section, we will delve into the mining basics, exploring the concepts of proof-of-work, mining hardware, mining pools, and the role of miners in maintaining the network. Understanding mining is crucial for comprehending the robustness and sustainability of the cryptocurrency ecosystem.

In the context of cryptocurrencies like Bitcoin, mining is the procedure that adds new blocks to the blockchain and verifies new transactions. Miners are essential to maintaining network security and confirming the authenticity of transactions. Proof-of-work (PoW) is the process of mining, which entails leveraging processing power to solve difficult mathematical puzzles. A miner receives payment in the form of freshly created cryptocurrency coins and transaction fees after they solve the problem and upload a new block of transactions to the blockchain.

The consensus method employed by Bitcoin and several other cryptocurrencies is called proof-of-work. Miners need to figure out this cryptographic puzzle in order to add new blocks to the network. The puzzle is computationally intensive and requires substantial computational power. Miners compete with each other to find a solution to the puzzle, and the first one to do so gets the right to add the next block and claim the block reward.

The complexity of the PoW puzzle is adjustable and is designed to maintain a consistent block generation time, usually around 10 minutes for Bitcoin. As more miners participate in the network, the overall computational power increases, and the difficulty of the PoW puzzle is automatically adjusted to ensure that blocks are generated at a predictable rate.

Mining hardware is a crucial aspect of the mining process. The computational power and efficiency of the mining hardware significantly impact a miner's ability to compete and successfully solve the PoW puzzle. In the early days of Bitcoin, miners used regular CPUs (Central Processing Units) to mine coins. However, as the network grew and the difficulty increased, CPUs became insufficient, leading to the development of more powerful mining hardware. Today, specialized hardware known as Application-Specific Integrated Circuits (ASICs) are commonly used for mining. ASICs are specifically designed to perform the mathematical calculations required for mining, making them much more efficient and powerful than general-purpose CPUs or GPUs (Graphics Processing Units). The use of ASICs has significantly increased the overall computational power of the network, making it more secure and competitive.

As the mining difficulty has risen over the years, individual miners face significant challenges in successfully mining blocks on their own. The probability of a single miner solving the PoW puzzle and adding a block to the chain decreases as more miners join the network. To address this, miners often join mining pools.

To improve their odds of effectively mining a block, miners form mining pools and pool their resources and computational power. Based on each member's contribution to the pool's processing capacity, the reward is divided among all members when a mining pool successfully mines a block. Joining a mining pool allows smaller miners to receive more consistent rewards, albeit at a slightly lower payout per individual compared to solo mining. Additionally, mining pools enhance the overall network security by ensuring that no single entity or group controls a significant portion of the mining power.

Miners are crucial in maintaining the integrity and security of the blockchain network. They validate and process transactions, ensuring that double-spending or fraudulent activities are prevented. When a user starts a Bitcoin transaction, it is announce to the network and enters a pool of unconfirmed transactions known as the mempool. Miners select transactions from the mempool and include them in the next block they aim to mine. They prioritize transactions with higher transaction fees, as these incentivize miners to include them in the block. By solving the PoW puzzle and successfully adding a block to the blockchain, miners confirm the validity of the included transactions, making them irreversible and adding them to the immutable public ledger.

The process of mining not only validates transactions but also ensures the decentralization and security of the network. As more miners participate, the network becomes more decentralized, reducing the risk of any single entity gaining control over the majority of the computational power (a situation known as a 51% attack). The decentralized nature of the network makes it resistant to censorship and ensures that no single entity can manipulate the transaction history or control the supply of the cryptocurrency.

As a payment for their efforts, miners receive block rewards and transaction fees for successfully mining a block. The block reward is a predetermined number of newly minted coins, and it serves as the mechanism by which new coins are introduced into circulation. In the case of Bitcoin, the initial block reward was 50 BTC, but it undergoes a halving event approximately every four years, reducing the block reward by half. The latest block reward after the 2020 halving is 6.25 BTC.

Miners also acquire transaction fees for including transactions in the blocks they mine. Users can voluntarily attach transaction fees to their transactions as an incentive for miners to prioritize them. Higher transaction fees increase the possibility that a miner will entail the transaction in their block.

Bitcoin's block reward undergoes a halving event approximately every four years, or after every 210,000 blocks mined. This halving reduces the block reward by half. The halving is a fundamental aspect of Bitcoin's monetary policy and is designed to limit the total supply of coins to 21 million, making Bitcoin a deflationary asset. The halving has significant implications for miners and the overall mining economics. After each halving, the block reward is reduced, and miners receive fewer newly minted coins as a reward for their efforts. This reduction in block rewards affects miner profitability, as they must rely more on transaction fees to sustain their operations. As the block reward decreases over time, miners face increasing pressure to operate efficiently and reduce operational costs. Additionally, the reduction in block rewards can impact the overall supply dynamics of the cryptocurrency, potentially leading to increased scarcity and upward price pressure.

The process of mining, particularly using energy-intensive ASICs, consumes a considerable amount of electricity. As the Bitcoin network has grown and mining has become more competitive, the energy consumption associated with mining has also increased significantly. This has raised concerns about the impact of mining in the environment, particularly when a significant portion of mining operations rely on fossil fuels for energy.

Critics argue that the energy consumption of mining is wasteful and unsustainable, as it contributes to greenhouse gas emissions and environmental degradation. However, proponents of Bitcoin and mining point out that mining is a competitive process, and miners naturally gravitate toward using energy sources that are cost-effective and efficient.

Efforts are being made to explore more sustainable and energy-efficient mining practices, such as utilizing renewable energy sources like hydro, solar, or wind power. Additionally, some mining operations are located in regions with excess energy capacity, where mining can help utilize otherwise wasted energy.

Mining is an essential process that contributes to the functionality, security, and decentralization of the blockchain network. Through proof-of-work, miners validate transactions, add new blocks to the chain, and guarantee the integrity of the entire system. The use of specialized mining hardware, mining pools, and the role of miners in maintaining the network's decentralization are critical aspects of the mining process.

Block rewards and transaction fees serve as incentives for miners to participate in the network and validate transactions. Halving events affect miner profitability and have implications for the overall supply dynamics of the cryptocurrency. As the network continues to grow, efforts to explore more sustainable and energy-efficient mining practices will play a vital role in mitigating concerns about the environmental impact of mining.

Mining is an integral part of the cryptocurrency ecosystem, and its continued development and innovation are essential for the sustainability and evolution of blockchain technology. Understanding mining basics is crucial for investors, enthusiasts, and policymakers alike as they navigate the complex world of cryptocurrencies and blockchain networks. As the technology continues to mature, mining will likely remain a fundamental and ever-evolving aspect of the cryptocurrency landscape.

Mining hardware and software requirements

Bitcoin mining plays a fundamental role in the operation and security of the Bitcoin network. Miners solve difficult mathematical puzzles, verify transactions, and add fresh blocks to the blockchain using specialized technology and software. Mining has changed from being a recreational activity to an extremely competitive and professional sector as the Bitcoin network has matured. In this section, we will explore the hardware and software requirements for Bitcoin mining, the technological advancements that have shaped the industry, and the challenges faced by miners in this ever-evolving landscape.

In the early days of Bitcoin, mining could be done effectively on personal computers or basic CPUs (Central Processing Units). However, as the network's difficulty increased, and the competition intensified, more powerful hardware was required to remain profitable. Today, Bitcoin mining predominantly relies on specialized hardware known as Application-Specific Integrated Circuits (ASICs). ASICs are designed only for the purpose of mining cryptocurrencies and can perform the required calculations at a much higher efficiency compared to general-purpose CPUs or GPUs (Graphics Processing Units).

ASICs are designed with custom-built chips optimized for performing the SHA-256 hashing algorithm used in

Bitcoin mining. These chips are highly energy-efficient and can perform trillions of calculations per second, significantly increasing the chances of successfully mining a block. The hash rate, measured in hashes per second (H/s), indicates the mining power of a hardware device, with higher hash rates equating to more efficient mining capabilities.

ASIC miners come in various shapes and sizes, ranging from small USB miners to massive data center-sized rigs. Miners can purchase individual ASIC devices or join mining pools, where multiple miners combine their hash power to increase their chances of mining a block and share the rewards.

The history of Bitcoin mining hardware is marked by a series of technological advancements that have shaped the industry's landscape. In the early days, CPU mining was quickly surpassed by GPU mining, which provided significantly better hash rates and energy efficiency. GPU mining became the standard for a brief period until the advent of FPGA (Field-Programmable Gate Array) miners, which offered even greater efficiency and hash rates.

However, the real game-changer came with the introduction of ASICs. In 2013, the first ASIC miners were released, offering hash rates hundreds of times more efficient than GPUs. This shift in mining hardware marked the beginning of an industrial-scale mining race, as mining farms equipped with ASICs dominated the network, leaving hobbyist miners at a significant disadvantage.

Over the years, ASIC technology has continued to advance, leading to ever more powerful and energy-efficient miners. Manufacturers compete to develop the most advanced ASICs, with each new generation outperforming the previous one. As a result, mining has become increasingly competitive, requiring constant hardware upgrades to remain profitable.

In addition to specialized hardware, miners also require software to connect their mining devices to the Bitcoin network and participate in the mining process effectively. Mining software serves as the interface between the mining hardware and the Bitcoin network, handling the communication and coordination necessary to validate transactions and add new blocks to the blockchain.

Mining software is generally open-source, and there are various options available, each with its unique features and customization options. Some popular mining software includes CGMiner, BFGMiner, and Easyminer, among others. When selecting mining software, miners consider factors such as compatibility with their ASIC hardware, ease of use, stability, and the level of technical support provided.

As the mining difficulty has increased and individual miners find it increasingly challenging to mine blocks independently, mining pools have emerged as a popular alternative. Mining pools are associations of miners who combine their hash power, allowing them to collectively mine blocks and share the rewards based on each miner's contributed hash rate.

Mining pools use specialized pool software that manages the distribution of work among participants, verifies submitted shares, and calculates each miner's share of the block reward. Popular pool software includes Stratum, Slush Pool, F2Pool, and Antpool. Miners can choose from a variety of pools based on factors such as pool fees, payout methods, and the pool's reputation.

Mining pools have become an essential part of the mining ecosystem, providing smaller miners with a chance to participate in block rewards and smoothing out the income for all participants. Pool mining allows miners to receive more frequent payouts, reducing the variance associated with individual mining.

While Bitcoin mining can be profitable, it is not without its challenges and considerations. Mining hardware is expensive, and with the rapid pace of technological advancements, miners must continually upgrade their equipment to remain competitive. Additionally, the energy consumption associated with mining can be substantial, leading to high operational costs, especially in regions with expensive electricity.

The competition among miners has intensified, making it more challenging for individual miners to compete against large mining farms. As mining difficulty increases, miners must continually increase their hash power to maintain their share of the network's total mining power.

Another critical consideration for miners is the issue of centralization. The increasing dominance of large mining farms and pools raises concerns about the concentration of hash power in the hands of a few entities. This concentration could potentially lead to a 51% attack, where a malicious actor gains control of the majority of the network's hash power and can manipulate transactions or double-spend coins. However, the decentralized nature of Bitcoin's mining community has so far prevented any such attack from occurring.

Bitcoin mining has developed significantly since its inception, transitioning from CPU mining to GPU mining and eventually to specialized ASIC mining. The development of ASICs has driven the industrialization of mining, with large-scale mining farms dominating the network. Mining software and pools have facilitated the participation of smaller miners, allowing them to earn more consistent rewards.

As the Bitcoin network continues to grow, miners must adapt to new technological advancements and the ever-increasing mining difficulty. The challenges of high hardware costs, energy consumption, and centralization concerns continue to shape the mining landscape.

Despite these challenges, Bitcoin mining remains a crucial process that secures the network and validates transactions. As the cryptocurrency ecosystem continues to evolve, miners will be vital in maintaining the integrity and security of the Bitcoin network, ensuring its continued success as a decentralized and trustless financial system.

The halving process and its impact on rewards

The world's first and most popular cryptocurrency, Bitcoin, operates on a unique monetary policy that includes a process known as "halving." The halving process is an essential feature of Bitcoin's design, designed to control the issuance rate and total supply of the digital currency. In this section, we will delve into the concept of halving, its historical significance, and its impact on the rewards received by miners. Understanding the halving process is crucial for investors, miners, and enthusiasts alike, as it plays a significant role in shaping the economics and future of Bitcoin.

To comprehend the halving process, one must first grasp the foundational principles of Bitcoin. Created in 2008 by an anonymous individual or group known as Satoshi Nakamoto, Bitcoin was introduced as an alternative to traditional fiat currencies. It aimed to address the issues of trust and centralization associated with traditional financial systems by leveraging blockchain technology.

The blockchain is an immutable and decentralized public ledger that records all Bitcoin transactions. Miners validate and add new transactions to the blockchain by solving complex mathematical puzzles through a process called proof-of-work. As a reward for their efforts and the computational power expended, miners receive newly minted bitcoins and transaction fees.

The halving process is a central aspect of Bitcoin's monetary policy, contributing to its deflationary nature. It is programmed into the Bitcoin protocol and occurs almost every four years or after every 210,000 blocks mined. During each halving event, the block reward received by miners is reduced by half.

In 2009, Bitcoin was first launched and miners received a block reward of 50 bitcoins for every block they mined. The first halving occurred in 2012, reducing the block reward to 25 bitcoins. The second halving took place in 2016, reducing the block reward further to 12.5 bitcoins. Subsequent halvings have continued to reduce the block reward, with the most recent halving occurring in 2020, reducing the reward to 6.25 bitcoins.
The halving process continues until the maximum supply of 21 million bitcoins is reached, which is expected to occur in the year 2140. At that point, no more bitcoins will be mined, making it a truly scarce and finite digital asset.

The halving process is a fundamental mechanism that impacts the supply and demand of Bitcoin. On the supply side, the reduction in the block reward decreases the rate at which new bitcoins are introduced into the market. This reduction in the rate of issuance contributes to Bitcoin's scarcity and limited supply, aligning it with traditional precious metals like gold.

As the supply of new bitcoins decreases over time, the rate of inflation also decreases. In contrast, traditional fiat currencies are subject to inflationary pressures due to central banks' ability to print more money. The fixed supply and controlled issuance rate of Bitcoin make it an appealing option for those seeking an alternative store of value and a hedge against inflation.

Halving events have historically been related to the significant price movements in Bitcoin's price. Prior to each halving, there is often a period of heightened speculation and anticipation, with many investors and traders trying to predict the impact of the halving on the price.

The first halving in 2012 was followed by a significant increase in the price of Bitcoin, with the asset experiencing its first notable bull run. Similarly, the second halving in 2016 was followed by an even more substantial price surge, propelling Bitcoin to new all-time highs.

The most recent halving in 2020 was no exception, as it coincided with a surge in interest from institutional investors and increased adoption by mainstream companies. This led to a remarkable bull run in late 2020 and early 2021, culminating in Bitcoin reaching its highest price to date.

It is important to note that while halving events have been correlated with price increases in the past, there are numerous other factors at play in the cryptocurrency market. External events, macroeconomic factors, regulatory developments, and investor sentiment all contribute to the price movements of Bitcoin and other cryptocurrencies.

The halving process directly impacts miner rewards, as it reduces the number of bitcoins miners receive for each block they successfully mine. As mentioned earlier, when Bitcoin was first introduced, miners received a block reward of 50 bitcoins. Following the first halving, this reward was reduced to 25 bitcoins, then to 12.5 bitcoins, and finally to 6.25 bitcoins after the most recent halving. As

the block reward decreases, miners' revenue from block rewards diminishes unless there is a corresponding increase in the price of Bitcoin. A decrease in miner rewards can significantly affect mining profitability, especially for miners with high operational costs, such as electricity and maintenance expenses.

To maintain profitability after each halving, miners often seek to optimize their operations and reduce costs. This can involve upgrading to more efficient mining hardware, locating operations in regions with cheaper electricity, or joining mining pools to combine computational power and increase the chances of successfully mining blocks.

To ensure that new blocks are added to the blockchain at a relatively consistent rate, the Bitcoin protocol incorporates a mechanism known as the mining difficulty adjustment. This difficulty adjustment occurs approximately every two weeks and is designed to keep the average block time close to 10 minutes.

As miners join or leave the network, the total computational power dedicated to mining Bitcoin fluctuates. If too many miners are participating, blocks would be mined too quickly, leading to a decrease in the mining difficulty. Conversely, if too many miners leave the network, blocks would be mined too slowly, resulting in an increase in the mining difficulty.

The mining difficulty adjustment seeks to strike a balance, ensuring that new blocks are added to the blockchain at a stable and predictable rate. After each halving event, there is usually a period of adjustment as miners' revenues decrease, leading some less efficient miners to leave the network.

The halving process has significant long-term implications for Bitcoin's value proposition and its potential to serve as a store of value. With a fixed supply and a predictable issuance rate, Bitcoin is immune to the inflationary pressures that affect traditional fiat currencies.

This scarcity and predictable supply schedule are often cited as key attributes that make Bitcoin a compelling hedge against inflation and economic uncertainty. Additionally, the halving process fosters a sense of digital gold, where Bitcoin's limited supply and increasing scarcity make it comparable to traditional precious metals as a store of value.

As the mining rewards continue to decrease over time, the reliance on transaction fees to incentivize miners becomes more critical. Transaction fees are voluntarily attached by users to their transactions as an incentive for miners to include them in the blocks they mine. As the proportion of block rewards relative to transaction fees decreases, transaction fees will play a more significant role in miner revenue.

Maintaining the safety and integrity of the Bitcoin network depends heavily on the halving process. The block reward serves as the primary incentive for miners to dedicate computational power and resources to the network. By reducing the block reward, the halving process challenges miners to optimize their operations continually.

This ongoing competition among miners ensures that the network remains decentralized and secure. In a decentralized system like Bitcoin, no single entity or group can control the majority of the network's hash rate. If any one entity were to gain such control, it could potentially undermine the network's security and integrity through a 51% attack.

By periodically reducing the block reward, the halving process encourages miners to continuously upgrade their hardware and look for more efficient and cost-effective ways to mine. This competition for rewards strengthens the overall security of the network, making it more robust against potential attacks.

CHAPTER VI

Bitcoin Regulation and Legal Considerations

Global regulatory landscape for Bitcoin

Bitcoin, as the pioneering cryptocurrency, has disrupted traditional financial systems and sparked a global conversation about the future of money and decentralized finance. As the popularity and adoption of Bitcoin have grown, so too have regulatory efforts by governments around the world to address the challenges and opportunities presented by this new digital asset. In this section, we will explore the global regulatory landscape for Bitcoin, examining the diverse approaches taken by different countries and international bodies. Understanding the regulatory environment is crucial for investors, businesses, and individuals engaging with Bitcoin to ensure compliance and navigate the legal complexities surrounding this revolutionary technology.

Bitcoin's decentralized and pseudonymous nature presents unique challenges for regulators. Unlike traditional financial systems, where intermediaries and authorities can monitor and control transactions, Bitcoin works on a peer-to-peer network, enabling users to transact directly without the need for third-party oversight. This lack of centralized control raises concerns about financial crime, tax evasion, and money laundering, prompting governments to grapple with ways to regulate Bitcoin without stifling innovation and technological progress.

Furthermore, the global nature of Bitcoin means that its use and impact transcend national borders, making a cohesive regulatory approach difficult to achieve. The diverse legal and regulatory frameworks across countries have led to fragmented and sometimes conflicting approaches to Bitcoin regulation, creating uncertainty for businesses and users seeking to operate on a global scale.

Several countries have taken a proactive approach to Bitcoin regulation by recognizing it as a legitimate form of currency or asset. Such recognition provides clarity for businesses and users, fostering a conducive environment for investment and innovation. For example, Japan has classified Bitcoin as legal tender, allowing businesses to accept it as payment and establishing a licensing framework for cryptocurrency exchanges.

Similarly, Switzerland has embraced Bitcoin as a legal asset, with its Financial Market Supervisory Authority (FINMA) providing guidelines for ICOs (Initial Coin Offerings) and cryptocurrency-related businesses. By acknowledging Bitcoin's existence and outlining regulatory guidelines, these countries seek to strike a balance between fostering innovation and ensuring consumer protection.

Some countries have adopted regulatory sandboxes, allowing companies and startups to experiment with blockchain technology and cryptocurrencies within a controlled and supervised environment. Regulatory sandboxes provide a space for businesses to develop and test new solutions while receiving regulatory support and feedback.

The United Kingdom, for instance, has implemented a regulatory sandbox under its Financial Conduct Authority (FCA), allowing companies to test innovative financial products and services, including those involving cryptocurrencies. These sandboxes help regulators better understand the technology's potential benefits and risks while allowing businesses to operate with a degree of flexibility not available under strict regulatory frameworks.

Taxation of cryptocurrencies has been a major focus for regulators. Different countries have adopted various approaches to taxing Bitcoin transactions, capital gains, and mining activities. Some treat Bitcoin as a form of currency, subjecting it to goods and services tax (GST) or value-added tax (VAT) upon purchase. Others treat it as a property, imposing capital gains tax on profits that were made from Bitcoin trading.

The Internal Revenue Service (or IRS) in the United States, for instance, considers Bitcoin and other cryptocurrencies as property for tax purposes. This means that individuals are required to report any gains or losses from Bitcoin transactions, and businesses must comply with tax regulations when accepting Bitcoin as payment for goods or services.

To address concerns about money laundering and illicit activities, many countries have implemented Anti-Money Laundering (AML) and Know Your Customer (KYC) regulations for cryptocurrency-related businesses. These regulations require businesses, including cryptocurrency exchanges and wallet providers, to confirm the identities of their customers and report suspicious activities to relevant authorities.

The European Union's Fifth Anti-Money Laundering Directive (AMLD5) extended AML regulations to cover cryptocurrency exchanges and wallet providers. Similarly, the Financial Crimes Enforcement Network (FinCEN) in the United States has issued guidance on AML requirements for virtual currency businesses.

On the other end of the spectrum, some countries have taken a more restrictive approach by outright banning or severely limiting the use and trading of cryptocurrencies.

China, for instance, has imposed strict restrictions on cryptocurrency trading and ICOs, banning cryptocurrency exchanges and initial coin offerings altogether.

India also proposed a bill to launch a central bank digital currency and ban private cryptocurrencies. These bans often stem from concerns about financial stability, consumer protection, and the potential for illicit activities. Given the global nature of cryptocurrencies, international coordination and cooperation are essential in effectively regulating Bitcoin and other digital assets. Various international bodies, such as the Financial Action Task Force (FATF), have issued guidelines and recommendations to assist countries in developing coherent and consistent regulatory frameworks.

The FATF's recommendations address AML and counter-terrorism financing (CFT) measures related to virtual assets and virtual asset service providers (VASPs). Countries are encouraged to implement these recommendations to mitigate the risks associated with cryptocurrency transactions while promoting a fair and transparent regulatory environment.

Despite efforts to regulate Bitcoin, significant challenges remain. The rapid pace advancements in technology and the decentralized nature of cryptocurrencies make it challenging for regulators to keep pace with developments and adapt their approaches accordingly. This creates a regulatory lag that can lead to uncertainties and legal ambiguities.

Moreover, the diverse and sometimes conflicting approaches taken by different countries can lead to regulatory arbitrage, where businesses choose to operate in jurisdictions with more favorable regulations. This can result in a race to the bottom, with countries competing to attract cryptocurrency businesses, potentially sacrificing consumer protection and systemic stability.

Looking ahead, the global regulatory landscape for Bitcoin will likely continue to evolve. As governments and international bodies gain a deeper understanding of the technology's potential and risks, more coherent and consistent regulatory frameworks may emerge. Striking a balance between innovation, consumer protection, and financial stability will remain a priority for regulators worldwide.

Taxation implications of owning and trading Bitcoin

Bitcoin, the revolutionary decentralized cryptocurrency, has gained significant popularity and adoption over the years. As more individuals and businesses engage with Bitcoin, it becomes essential to understand the taxation implications surrounding its ownership and trading. The unique characteristics of Bitcoin, such as its digital nature, pseudonymous transactions, and decentralized framework, present challenges for tax authorities worldwide. In this section, we will explore the taxation implications of owning and trading Bitcoin, examining how different countries approach the taxation of cryptocurrencies and the importance of complying with tax regulations to avoid legal and financial consequences.

One of the key questions surrounding the taxation of Bitcoin is its classification for tax purposes. Different countries have taken various approaches to this matter, leading to differences in how Bitcoin is taxed. Some countries treat Bitcoin as a form of currency, subjecting it to goods and services tax (GST) or value-added tax (VAT) upon purchase. In such cases, using Bitcoin for transactions can trigger tax implications similar to using fiat currency.

Other countries treat Bitcoin as property, similar to an asset like stocks or real estate. This means that the gains or losses made from purchasing and selling Bitcoin are subject to capital gains tax. For example, the Internal

Revenue Service (IRS) in the United States considers Bitcoin and other cryptocurrencies as property, requiring individuals to report capital gains and losses from Bitcoin transactions in their tax returns.

The tax classification of Bitcoin has a significant impact on how individuals and businesses need to report and calculate their tax liabilities, making it crucial to understand the specific regulations in each jurisdiction.

If someone owns Bitcoin as an investment, any increase in its value upon selling it or exchanging it for fiat money or other assets will be liable to capital gains tax. The difference between the acquisition price (cost basis) and the selling price of the Bitcoin is used to compute capital gains tax.

In general, long-term capital gains—which, in certain countries, apply to assets held for more than a year—are taxed at a lower rate compared with short-term capital gains, which are applicable to assets held for less than a year. The tax rates and holding periods for capital gains tax can vary significantly from one country to another, so it is crucial for Bitcoin holders to be aware of the tax rules in their respective jurisdictions.

Gifting Bitcoin to another individual may also have tax implications. In some countries, gifting Bitcoin may be subject to gift tax if the value of the gifted cryptocurrency exceeds a certain threshold. The gift tax rules and thresholds can vary depending on the country's tax laws

In the case of inheritance or bequeathing Bitcoin, it is essential to consider the inheritance tax regulations in the relevant jurisdiction. In some countries, inherited Bitcoin may be subject to inheritance tax based on its value at the time of inheritance.

For individuals and businesses engaged in active and frequent Bitcoin trading as a business, the profits derived from trading activities may be treated as business income. In such cases, the individual or business is required to report the profits and losses from trading as part of their regular income tax filings.

Trading as a business may also allow traders to deduct business-related expenses, such as trading fees and software costs, from their taxable income, potentially reducing their overall tax liability.

The frequency of Bitcoin trading can also impact how it is taxed. Day trading, where individuals buy and sell Bitcoin multiple times within a single day, may be subject to different tax treatment than occasional or infrequent trading.

In some jurisdictions, day trading may be classified as a form of business income, subject to higher tax rates and additional reporting requirements. Traders should be aware of the tax implications of their trading activities and keep accurate records of their transactions to make sure the compliance with tax regulations.

Bitcoin traders who incur losses from their trading activities may be able to offset these losses against their other income or future trading profits. This allows traders to reduce their taxable income and potentially receive tax benefits for their trading losses.

However, the specific rules regarding the treatment of trading losses can vary from one country to another, and some jurisdictions may impose limitations on the amount of losses that can be offset against other income.

Complying with tax regulations related to Bitcoin ownership and trading is essential to avoid legal and financial consequences. The decentralized and pseudonymous nature of Bitcoin transactions does not exempt individuals or businesses from tax obligations. Failure to report Bitcoin-related income or gains can lead to fines, penalties, as well as legal action by tax authorities.

To ensure compliance, Bitcoin owners and traders should maintain accurate records of all transactions, including dates, prices, and the counterparties involved. Additionally, they should stay informed about the tax regulations in their respective jurisdictions, as tax laws regarding cryptocurrencies are continuously evolving.

Some countries have introduced specific guidance on the taxation of cryptocurrencies, while others may issue updates or amendments to existing tax codes to address the unique challenges posed by digital assets. Seeking advice from tax professionals familiar with cryptocurrency taxation can be beneficial in navigating the complexities of Bitcoin taxation.

The taxation of Bitcoin varies significantly from country to country, reflecting the diverse approaches taken by different governments to regulate cryptocurrencies. While some countries have embraced Bitcoin and implemented clear tax guidelines, others have taken a more cautious or restrictive approach.

For example, in Germany, Bitcoin is treated as private money, exempting it from VAT when used for payments. However, profits from Bitcoin trading are subject to capital gains tax. In Australia, Bitcoin is considered property, and transactions involving Bitcoin are subject to GST.

On the other hand, some countries, such as Bolivia and Algeria, have imposed outright bans on the use of Bitcoin and other cryptocurrencies, making taxation irrelevant in such jurisdictions.

As the adoption of Bitcoin and other cryptocurrencies grows on a global scale, there is a growing need for international cooperation and harmonization of tax regulations. The decentralized and borderless nature of cryptocurrencies means that transactions can occur across jurisdictions, making it challenging for tax authorities to effectively track and regulate cryptocurrency-related income and gains.

International bodies, like the G20 and Organization for Economic Cooperation and Development (or OECD), have recognized the importance of addressing the tax implications of cryptocurrencies. These bodies have initiated discussions on creating a cohesive and standardized approach to cryptocurrency taxation to impede regulatory arbitrage and guarantee a level playing field for businesses and individuals worldwide.

AML (Anti-Money Laundering) and KYC (Know Your Customer) requirements

Concerns over Bitcoin and other cryptocurrencies' possible use for illegal motives, like money laundering and financing terrorists, have grown in importance as they have been more widely accepted. In response to these concerns, regulatory authorities around the world have implemented Anti-Money Laundering (AML) and Know Your Customer (KYC) requirements for businesses operating in the cryptocurrency space. These requirements aim to enhance transparency, traceability, and accountability in cryptocurrency transactions while mitigating the risks of financial crime. In this section, we will explore the AML and KYC requirements in the context of Bitcoin, examining their importance, challenges, and impact on the cryptocurrency ecosystem.

Money laundering is the process of disguising the origins of illegally obtained funds to make them appear legitimate. Criminals engage in money laundering to avoid detection and prosecution by law enforcement authorities. The use of cryptocurrencies, including Bitcoin, has been seen as a potential avenue for money launderers due to the pseudonymous nature of blockchain transactions, which can conceal the identities of the parties involved.

To address the risks of money laundering and other financial crimes in the cryptocurrency industry, many countries have implemented AML regulations that apply to cryptocurrency-related businesses. These regulations require these businesses to implement robust AML programs, perform due diligence on their customers, as well as report suspicious activities to relevant authorities.

For instance, the Financial Crimes Enforcement Network (or FinCEN) in the United States, issued guidance in 2013 stating that virtual currency exchanges and administrators are considered Money Services Businesses (MSBs) and must register with FinCEN. Additionally, they are subject to AML regulations, including the reporting of suspicious activity reports (or SARs) and currency transaction reports (or CTRs).

The decentralized and pseudonymous nature of Bitcoin transactions presents unique challenges for AML compliance. Unlike traditional financial institutions, cryptocurrency transactions occur directly between users, making it more challenging for authorities to identify the parties involved.

Cryptocurrency mixers and tumblers, which combine transactions from multiple users to obfuscate the trail of funds, can further complicate AML efforts. Criminals may exploit these services to launder money and make the tracing of illicit funds more difficult for law enforcement agencies.

To meet AML requirements, cryptocurrency businesses must implement enhanced due diligence measures and verify the identities of their customers. This involves collecting and verifying personal information, such as government-issued identification and proof of address, to establish the customer's identity and ensure compliance with AML regulations.

Cryptocurrency exchanges and other service providers often employ automated identity verification processes and conduct transaction monitoring to detect suspicious activities. Large or unusual transactions may trigger additional scrutiny, requiring users to provide further documentation to explain the origin and purpose of the funds.

Know Your Customer (KYC) is a process through which businesses verify their customers identity and assess their risk profiles. KYC procedures are an important part of AML efforts, as they enable businesses to better understand their customers, identify high-risk individuals or entities, and prevent potential misuse of their services for illegal activities.

In the cryptocurrency space, KYC requirements are particularly important for cryptocurrency exchanges, wallet providers, and other platforms that facilitate the conversion between cryptocurrencies and fiat currencies. By knowing their customers and understanding their financial activities, these businesses can detect and report suspicious transactions more effectively.

KYC regulations in the cryptocurrency industry vary from one country to another, with some jurisdictions imposing more stringent requirements than others. While some countries have clear guidelines for cryptocurrency businesses, others are still in the process of developing or refining their regulatory frameworks.

Countries like Japan and Switzerland have introduced comprehensive KYC regulations for cryptocurrency exchanges and service providers to ensure compliance with AML standards. These regulations include customer verification, transaction monitoring, and reporting suspicious activities to the relevant authorities.

One of the primary concerns raised by KYC requirements in the cryptocurrency space is the potential compromise of user privacy and data security. Requiring individuals to provide sensitive personal information to cryptocurrency businesses raises concerns about the confidentiality and protection of that data.

Cryptocurrency companies must strike a balance between complying with regulatory requirements and safeguarding customer privacy. Implementing robust data security measures and ensuring that customer information is handled responsibly and transparently are essential for building trust with users.

The implementation of AML and KYC requirements in the cryptocurrency industry has contributed to increased transparency and legitimacy. By adopting AML and KYC practices, cryptocurrency businesses demonstrate their commitment to hindering financial crime and operating within the bounds of the law.

This increased transparency can also foster greater trust and confidence among users, investors, and regulatory authorities, encouraging broader adoption and investment in the cryptocurrency ecosystem.

While AML and KYC requirements are necessary for combating money laundering and ensuring regulatory compliance, they can also impose significant costs and operational burdens on cryptocurrency businesses, particularly smaller startups and companies with limited resources.

Complying with AML and KYC regulations may involve investing in sophisticated identity verification systems, hiring compliance officers, and conducting ongoing monitoring of customer transactions. These compliance costs can be particularly challenging for startups and may hinder innovation in the industry.

The cryptocurrency industry's global nature makes it challenging to achieve consistent and harmonized AML and KYC standards across different jurisdictions. The lack of global regulatory alignment can lead to regulatory arbitrage, where businesses choose to operate in countries with less stringent AML and KYC requirements to reduce compliance costs.

International coordination and cooperation among governments and regulatory bodies are essential to addressing the challenges posed by money laundering and other financial crimes in the cryptocurrency space. Organizations like Financial Action Task Force (FATF) are crucial in promoting international cooperation and developing AML and KYC standards for cryptocurrencies.

CHAPTER VII

Alternative Cryptocurrencies (Altcoins)

Understanding altcoins and their purpose

Any cryptocurrency other than Bitcoin is referred to as an altcoins, short for alternative coins. Although Bitcoin was the initial and most widely recognized cryptocurrency, a wide variety of altcoins have emerged as a result of the popularity of blockchain technology, which powers Bitcoin. Each altcoin serves a unique purpose and aims to address specific limitations or offer different features compared to Bitcoin. In this section, we will explore the concept of altcoins, their purposes, and the role they play in the broader cryptocurrency ecosystem.

The cryptocurrency era began with the creation of Bitcoin in 2009, which was created by the anonymous Satoshi Nakamoto. It introduced the concept of a decentralized, peer-to-peer digital currency, secured by blockchain technology. As Bitcoin gained popularity and its value surged over time, it became evident that the blockchain technology underlying Bitcoin had applications beyond digital currency.

Inspired by Bitcoin's success, developers and entrepreneurs began to experiment with variations of the Bitcoin codebase to create alternative cryptocurrencies. These alternative cryptocurrencies, or altcoins, sought to introduce innovations, improvements, or specific use cases that differentiated them from Bitcoin.

One of the primary areas of innovation for altcoins has been scalability. Bitcoin's original block size and block time limitations meant that it could process only a limited number of transactions per second, leading to network congestion and higher transaction fees during peak times. To address this limitation, altcoins like Litecoin and Bitcoin Cash were created with larger block sizes and faster block times, allowing them to handle more transactions per second.

Additionally, projects like Ethereum introduced the concept of smart contracts, which enabled programmable, self-executing agreements on the blockchain. This innovation opened up new possibilities for decentralized applications (dApps) and further expanded the use cases of blockchain technology beyond simple transactions.

Even though all Bitcoin transactions are publicly visible on the blockchain, some users might prefer more anonymity and privacy. Altcoins like Monero, Zcash, and Dash offer enhanced privacy features, such as ring signatures, zero-knowledge proofs, and optional privacy settings, allowing users to shield their transaction details from public view. These privacy-centric altcoins aim to address concerns about financial privacy and data protection, catering to users who prioritize anonymity in their cryptocurrency transactions.

Some altcoins were designed with specific use cases in mind, catering to niche markets or industries. For example, Ripple (XRP) was created as a digital payment protocol for banks and financial institutions, facilitating fast, low-cost cross-border transactions. Stellar (XLM) aims to provide affordable financial services to the unbanked and underbanked populations in developing countries.

Other altcoins, like Chainlink (LINK) and Aave (AAVE), focus on decentralized finance (DeFi) applications, enabling smart contracts to access real-world data and providing lending and borrowing services on the blockchain.

Altcoins have also experimented with different governance models to address issues related to decision-making and network upgrades. Some altcoins, like Decred (DCR) and Tezos (XTZ), utilize on-chain governance systems, where holders of the cryptocurrency can vote on proposals and changes to the protocol.

Others, like Cardano (ADA) and Polkadot (DOT), implement a more formalized governance structure, involving multiple stakeholders, research institutions, and developers to determine the network's future direction.

Altcoins are often referred to as "Bitcoin alternatives," but they are not necessarily in direct competition with Bitcoin. Instead, many altcoins aim to complement or enhance the capabilities of Bitcoin. They coexist with Bitcoin in the broader cryptocurrency ecosystem, each offering its unique value proposition.

Bitcoin's status as the first and most dominant cryptocurrency grants it a level of recognition and acceptance that many altcoins seek to achieve. As the market leader, Bitcoin has established itself as a store of value and a digital gold, appealing to investors seeking a hedge against inflation and economic uncertainty.

On the other hand, altcoins may offer technological innovations, improved transaction speeds, or additional functionalities that attract users with specific needs or preferences. Altcoins may also serve as experimental platforms, testing new ideas and technologies that could eventually be incorporated into the Bitcoin network if proven successful and secure.

While altcoins offer diverse opportunities and innovations, they also come with certain risks and challenges. The abundance of altcoins in the market can lead to a crowded and competitive landscape, making it challenging for individual projects to stand out and gain widespread adoption.

Investing in altcoins can be riskier compared to investing in Bitcoin due to their comparatively lower liquidity and market capitalization. Smaller altcoins may also be more susceptible to price manipulation and volatility, leading to potential losses for investors.

Furthermore, not all altcoin projects are genuine or viable in the long term. Some altcoins may be created as part of pump-and-dump schemes or fraudulent endeavors, aiming to capitalize on the hype surrounding cryptocurrency without delivering on their promises.

Investors and users interested in altcoins must exercise caution, conduct thorough research, and assess the credibility and legitimacy of the projects they are considering.

As the cryptocurrency space evolves, the role of altcoins remains a topic of debate and speculation. While Bitcoin's position as the market leader is unlikely to be challenged in the near term, altcoins will continue to play an essential role in driving innovation, experimentation, and diversity in the cryptocurrency ecosystem.

Some altcoins may gain widespread adoption and recognition, becoming influential players in their respective niches or industries. Others may fade away or consolidate as the market matures and the true value propositions of various projects become more evident.

Interoperability between different blockchains, such as through protocols like Polkadot and Cosmos, may enable altcoins to collaborate and leverage each other's strengths, further enhancing the overall capabilities of the cryptocurrency ecosystem.

Popular altcoins and their differences from Bitcoin

As the cryptocurrency market continues to grow, numerous altcoins have emerged alongside Bitcoin, each with its unique features and use cases. While Bitcoin remains the most recognized and dominant cryptocurrency, altcoins have captured significant attention and investment due to their potential for innovation and addressing specific limitations of Bitcoin. In this section, we will explore some popular altcoins and examine their differences from Bitcoin, highlighting their distinctive attributes and contributions to the broader cryptocurrency ecosystem.

Ethereum is arguably the most significant and influential altcoin after Bitcoin. Created by Vitalik Buterin in 2015, Ethereum introduced the idea of smart contracts, enabling developers to build decentralized applications (dApps) on its blockchain. Unlike Bitcoin, which primarily serves as digital gold and a medium of exchange, Ethereum's programmability and flexibility make it a versatile platform for various use cases beyond simple transactions.

Smart contracts on Ethereum allow for the creation of decentralized autonomous organizations (DAOs), non-fungible tokens (NFTs), and decentralized finance (DeFi) protocols, among other applications. The ability to execute code automatically without intermediaries has sparked a wave of innovation in the decentralized application space, attracting developers and projects seeking to disrupt traditional industries with blockchain technology.

Ripple, known for its digital payment protocol and native cryptocurrency XRP, aims to facilitate fast and low-cost cross-border transactions. Unlike numerous other cryptocurrencies like Bitcoin, Ripple is not based on a conventional blockchain. Rather, it uses a special consensus algorithm that enables higher scalability and faster transaction confirmation times.

The Ripple network is designed to bridge the gap between traditional financial institutions, enabling them to conduct efficient and cost-effective cross-border payments. The focus on remittances and international money transfers sets Ripple apart from Bitcoin, which primarily serves as a decentralized store of value and does not target the traditional banking sector.

As the "silver to Bitcoin's gold," Litecoin was among the first cryptocurrencies and is similar to Bitcoin in many ways. Litecoin was created by Charlie Lee in 2011, with the goal of being a quicker and lighter variant of Bitcoin. Compared to Bitcoin, which utilizes the SHA-256 mining algorithm, it uses Scrypt, which leads to faster block confirmation times and more transaction throughput.

While Litecoin's transaction speed and lower fees make it a popular choice for everyday transactions, its primary utility remains as a digital currency for peer-to-peer payments. Litecoin's close resemblance to Bitcoin makes it a less experimental choice for users looking for an alternative to Bitcoin without deviating significantly from the original cryptocurrency concept.

Bitcoin Cash is a result of a hard fork from the Bitcoin network that occurred in 2017. The fork was initiated to address concerns over Bitcoin's scalability and high transaction fees. Bitcoin Cash increased the block size up to 8MB, allowing for more transactions to be included in each block and reducing congestion on the network.
The larger block size and lower fees position Bitcoin Cash as a digital currency optimized for everyday transactions, aiming to fulfill Bitcoin's original vision as a peer-to-peer

electronic cash system. While it shares the same basic principles as Bitcoin, Bitcoin Cash emphasizes speed and affordability, catering to users who prioritize fast and cheap transactions.

A blockchain platform that focuses on sustainability, scalability, and peer-reviewed research is known as cardano. Created by a team of professionals and engineers, Cardano aims to offer a more rigorous approach to blockchain development. It employs a layered architecture, separating the settlement layer for transactions from the computation layer for smart contracts.

Cardano's research-driven approach and commitment to formal verification have attracted attention from institutions and enterprises interested in exploring blockchain technology. Unlike Bitcoin, which relies heavily on community-driven development, Cardano's academic approach sets it apart, positioning itself as a platform for building secure and reliable applications.

Polkadot is a multi-chain blockchain platform that facilitates interoperability between different blockchains. Created by Ethereum co-founder Gavin Wood, Polkadot's main goal is to address the issue of blockchain fragmentation by allowing independent blockchains to connect and interact with each other.

The Polkadot ecosystem operates on a relay chain that serves as the main chain, connecting various parachains (parallel chains) with different functionalities. This architecture enables Polkadot to scale efficiently and promote innovation through cross-chain communication. While Bitcoin operates as a single blockchain, Polkadot's focus on interoperability sets it apart as a network designed to foster collaboration and synergy between different blockchain projects.

The native coin of one of the biggest and most well-known cryptocurrency exchanges worldwide, Binance Exchange, is called Binance Coin. Initially launched as an ERC-20 token on the Ethereum blockchain, Binance Coin migrated to Binance's native blockchain, Binance Smart Chain (BSC), to facilitate faster and cheaper transactions.

Binance Coin serves multiple purposes, including paying for transaction fees on the Binance exchange, participating in token sales on the Binance Launchpad, and participating in decentralized finance (DeFi) protocols on BSC. The integration of Binance Coin within the Binance ecosystem makes it a valuable utility token, providing benefits and discounts to users within the platform.

The cryptocurrency ecosystem is vast and diverse, with a myriad of altcoins offering unique features, use cases, and approaches to blockchain technology. While Bitcoin remains the dominant force and digital gold of the crypto space, altcoins have demonstrated their potential to drive innovation and cater to specific needs and preferences of users.

Diversifying your cryptocurrency portfolio

Investing in cryptocurrencies has gained significant popularity as the digital asset class continues to demonstrate its potential for high returns. While Bitcoin remains the dominant and most well-known cryptocurrency, the market has expanded to entail a diverse range of altcoins with various use cases and value propositions. Diversifying your cryptocurrency portfolio is an essential strategy to manage risk and enhance potential returns. In this section, we will explore the concept of diversification, its benefits and challenges, and provide practical tips for constructing a well-diversified cryptocurrency portfolio.

As a risk management technique, diversification entails distributing investments among several asset classes or types of assets. The main objective of diversification is to make sure that possible losses from one investment are balanced out by gains from other assets, so lowering the overall risk of a portfolio. In the context of cryptocurrencies, diversification means holding a mix of different cryptocurrencies rather than investing solely in one or a few.

The cryptocurrency market is known for its high volatility and inherent risk, making diversification particularly relevant. By holding a variety of cryptocurrencies, investors can mitigate the impact of adverse price movements in any single asset and increase the potential for positive returns.

The main advantage of diversification is risk reduction. Cryptocurrencies can experience extreme price fluctuations due to factors like market sentiment, regulatory developments, technological advancements, and macroeconomic conditions. By spreading investments across different cryptocurrencies, investors reduce their exposure to the price movements of any single asset, thereby reducing the overall portfolio risk.

Each cryptocurrency offers a unique set of features, use cases, and potential for growth. By diversifying, investors gain exposure to a broader range of opportunities within the cryptocurrency ecosystem. For instance, holding cryptocurrencies with a focus on decentralized finance (DeFi), cross-border payments, privacy, or smart contracts provides exposure to different sectors of the blockchain industry.

Cryptocurrency markets often experience cycles of boom and bust, with different assets performing better at different times. By diversifying, investors can capitalize on these market cycles, positioning themselves to benefit from the growth of certain cryptocurrencies during bull markets and potentially protecting their capital during bear markets.

Diversifying a cryptocurrency portfolio requires thorough research and understanding of each asset. Investors need to assess the technology, use case, development team, community support, and potential risks associated with each cryptocurrency. Conducting this level of due diligence can be time-consuming and challenging, especially for newcomers to the cryptocurrency space.

As the number of cryptocurrencies in a portfolio increases, so does the difficulty of managing and securing the assets. Holding multiple cryptocurrencies on different wallets or exchanges can lead to security vulnerabilities. Investors must implement robust security measures, such as hardware wallets and two-factor authentication, to safeguard their diversified portfolio effectively.

Not all cryptocurrencies are equally liquid, meaning some may have reduced trading volumes and higher bid-ask spreads. In illiquid markets, buying or selling significant amounts of a cryptocurrency can impact the price, potentially leading to slippage. Additionally, some smaller altcoins may only be available on a limited number of exchanges, making them less accessible for investors.

Before constructing a diversified cryptocurrency portfolio, it is essential to define investment goals and risk tolerance. Different investors have varying objectives, such as capital appreciation, income generation, or long-term wealth preservation. Given that cryptocurrencies can be extremely volatile and that investors should be ready for the possibility of large price fluctuations, it is imperative that investors understand their risk tolerance.

A well-diversified cryptocurrency portfolio should include a mix of major cryptocurrencies, such as Bitcoin and Ethereum, and a selection of altcoins with different use cases and potential for growth. Major cryptocurrencies serve as the foundation of the portfolio, providing stability and liquidity, while altcoins offer opportunities for higher returns and exposure to emerging trends.

Market capitalization is a useful metric to consider when diversifying a cryptocurrency portfolio. Larger cryptocurrencies with higher market capitalization tend to be more established and have greater liquidity. Smaller-cap cryptocurrencies, while offering higher growth potential, may be more volatile and have higher risks. Investors should balance their exposure between established cryptocurrencies and promising smaller-cap projects based on their risk tolerance.

Thoroughly research the fundamentals and use cases of each cryptocurrency in the portfolio. Evaluate factors such as the strength of the development team, adoption, community support, partnerships, and real-world utility. Focus on projects with strong fundamentals and realistic use cases, as these are more likely to deliver sustainable value over time.

The cryptocurrency market is dynamic, with new projects emerging and existing ones evolving. Regularly rebalancing the portfolio helps maintain the desired asset allocation and guarantees that the portfolio remains aligned with investment goals. Rebalancing involves selling assets that have appreciated significantly and reinvesting the proceeds in underperforming assets to maintain the desired diversification.

Diversification alone may not completely eliminate risk. Investors should consider implementing risk management strategies, such as setting stop-loss orders or using position-sizing techniques, to limit potential losses and protect capital during market downturns.

As the cryptocurrency market continues to evolve, diversification will remain a vital strategy for investors seeking to navigate the ever-changing landscape and capitalize on the transformative potential of digital assets and blockchain technology.

CHAPTER VIII

Real-World Use Cases for Bitcoin

Bitcoin as a payment method

Bitcoin, the first and most well-known cryptocurrency, was initially envisioned as a peer-to-peer electronic cash system, allowing individuals to transact directly without the need for intermediaries like banks or payment processors. Over the years, Bitcoin has gained widespread recognition and acceptance as a store of value and investment asset. However, its potential as a payment method has been a topic of debate due to certain challenges and limitations. In this section, we will explore the use of Bitcoin as a payment method, examining its benefits, challenges, and the efforts to enhance its usability in everyday transactions.

One of the main advantages of utilizing Bitcoin for payments is its borderless nature. Traditional cross-border transactions often involve multiple intermediaries, leading to delays and higher fees. With Bitcoin, individuals can send and receive funds globally without the need for currency conversions or international banking channels. This feature makes Bitcoin an attractive option for remittances and international trade, particularly in regions with limited access to traditional banking services.

Compared to traditional payment methods, Bitcoin transactions typically involve lower fees. Bitcoin fees are decided by the size of the transaction and network demand, unlike traditional financial institutions that often charge a fixed fee or a percentage of the transaction amount. In some cases, Bitcoin fees can be significantly lower, making it an appealing option for microtransactions and small-value transfers.

Bitcoin has the potential to advance financial inclusion by giving the unbanked and underbanked populations access to financial services. A sizable segment of the general population lacks access to standard banking services in numerous places of the world. Bitcoin wallets can be created and accessed with only an internet connection, allowing individuals without a bank account to participate in the global economy.

Due to the use of cryptographic algorithms, Bitcoin transactions are extremely secure as well as resistant to fraud and chargebacks. A Bitcoin transaction cannot be undone or changed once it has been validated on the blockchain, giving retailers more security against payment-related threats. Additionally, users have full control over their Bitcoin funds, as they are not subject to the control of centralized financial institutions.

Bitcoin's decentralized nature allows for direct peer-to-peer transactions, eliminating the requirement for intermediaries like banks and payment processors. This disintermediation can lead to faster transactions and reduced reliance on centralized entities. Merchants accepting Bitcoin payments can also avoid payment processing fees and chargebacks associated with traditional payment methods.

Bitcoin's price volatility is one of the most significant challenges in using it as a payment method. The value of Bitcoin can fluctuate dramatically over short periods, making it challenging for buyers and sellers to determine the fair price of goods and services in Bitcoin terms. Merchants accepting Bitcoin payments may face exposure to exchange rate risk, leading to potential losses if they do not convert Bitcoin to fiat currency quickly.

Bitcoin's transaction processing time can vary based on network congestion and the transaction fee paid. During periods of high demand, transaction confirmation times can be delayed, leading to longer payment processing times for merchants and inconvenience for customers. The scalability issue and block size limitation of the Bitcoin network have resulted in slower transaction speeds compared to other cryptocurrencies and traditional payment systems.

Bitcoin transactions are irreversible, which means that once a payment is made, there is no recourse for consumers in cases of fraud or disputes. Unlike traditional payment methods that offer chargeback mechanisms and consumer protections, Bitcoin transactions do not have built-in mechanisms for resolving disputes. This lack of consumer protection may make some users hesitant to use Bitcoin for online purchases and transactions.

While the number of merchants accepting Bitcoin payments has grown over the years, it is still relatively small compared to traditional payment methods. Many businesses are cautious about accepting Bitcoin due to its price volatility and the challenges associated with accounting for cryptocurrency transactions. As a result, users may find it challenging to use Bitcoin for everyday purchases and services.

Despite the challenges, efforts are being made to enhance Bitcoin's usability as a payment method. Several solutions have been proposed and implemented to address issues like scalability and transaction speed:

A layer-2 scaling solution for Bitcoin that aims to enable faster and cheaper transactions, is known as the Lightning Network. It operates as an off-chain payment channel, allowing users to conduct multiple transactions without clogging the main Bitcoin blockchain. The Lightning Network can significantly improve the scalability and transaction speed of Bitcoin, making it more suitable for everyday microtransactions.

On the Bitcoin blockchain, Segregated Witness is a protocol update that maximizes transaction data storage and raises the block size limit. SegWit transactions occupy less space on the blockchain, enabling more transactions to be added in each block and reducing transaction fees. By adopting SegWit, users and merchants can enjoy faster and more cost-effective Bitcoin transactions. Several

financial companies offer Bitcoin debit cards that allow users to spend their Bitcoin holdings at merchants accepting traditional payment methods. These cards convert Bitcoin to fiat currency at the point of sale, enabling users to use Bitcoin for everyday purchases without directly exposing themselves to its price volatility. Payment processors and gateways provide services that facilitate Bitcoin payments for merchants. They often handle the conversion of Bitcoin to fiat currency, shielding merchants from the effects of price volatility. By integrating with existing payment systems, these services aim to make it easier for businesses to accept Bitcoin without the need for additional accounting or financial infrastructure.

Use cases in remittances and cross-border transactions

Bitcoin, the pioneering cryptocurrency, has garnered significant attention for its capacity to disrupt traditional financial systems and offer innovative solutions to various challenges. One area where Bitcoin has shown promise is in remittances and cross-border transactions. These transactions often involve high fees, long processing times, and limited accessibility to financial services, particularly in developing countries. In this section, we will explore how Bitcoin is being used as a viable alternative for remittances and cross-border transactions, highlighting its benefits, challenges, and potential impact on the global financial landscape.

A significant portion of the economies of many developing countries are reliant on the money that migrant workers send home to support their family. The World Bank estimates that in 2020, remittances to low- and middle-income nations will total more than $540 billion. However, traditional remittance channels are marred by various challenges, including high transaction fees, currency exchange costs, and delays in processing.

Cross-border transactions, whether for trade or international business, also face similar issues, making them costly and time-consuming for businesses and individuals alike. Banks and other financial institutions often act as intermediaries in these transactions, adding layers of bureaucracy and fees that can significantly impact the amount received by the recipient.

The possibility of reduced transaction fees when utilizing Bitcoin for cross-border and remittance transactions over more conventional means is one of the biggest benefits. The smallest transaction fee for sending Bitcoin abroad is usually only a little amount, much less than what banks and money transfer services charge. This cost-effectiveness can result in more funds reaching the intended recipients, particularly for smaller remittances. Bitcoin transactions are processed quickly, especially when compared to traditional cross-border transfers that can take several days to complete. Bitcoin transactions are typically confirmed on the blockchain within minutes, allowing recipients to access the funds more quickly. This speed can be particularly crucial in urgent situations or when the recipient requires immediate access to the funds.

Bitcoin offers a borderless and accessible solution for remittances and cross-border transactions. All that is required is an internet connection and a Bitcoin wallet, which can be set up by anyone with access to a smartphone or computer. In regions with insufficient access to traditional banking services, Bitcoin provides an opportunity for financial inclusion, allowing individuals to partake in the global economy without relying on traditional banking infrastructure.

Bitcoin transactions are secured through cryptographic techniques, providing a high level of security and transparency. The public nature of the blockchain ensures that transactions can be traced and verified, reducing the risk of fraud and ensuring transparency in the movement of funds. This feature is particularly valuable in cross-border transactions, where trust and transparency between parties may be challenging to establish.

For individuals sending money across borders, Bitcoin can also serve as a medium for currency conversion. Rather than using traditional exchange services with potentially unfavorable rates, Bitcoin enables individuals to convert their funds to the recipient's local currency directly. This can result in cost savings and more competitive exchange rates.

Bitcoin's price volatility is a significant concern in its use for remittances and cross-border transactions. The value of Bitcoin can change significantly over short periods, potentially leading to varying amounts received by recipients when converted to fiat currency. This price volatility poses risks for both senders and recipients, as the purchasing power of the funds may be affected during the time it takes to convert Bitcoin to local currency.

The regulatory landscape for cryptocurrencies, including Bitcoin, varies significantly from one country to another. Some countries have embraced cryptocurrencies and have established clear regulations, while others have imposed restrictions or outright bans on their use. The lack of a standardized regulatory framework can create uncertainty for businesses and individuals seeking to utilize Bitcoin for cross-border transactions.

Widespread adoption of Bitcoin for remittances and cross-border transactions remains a challenge. Many individuals and businesses may be hesitant to embrace Bitcoin due to its relatively nascent status and concerns about security and price volatility. Additionally, there is a need for education and awareness campaigns to inform potential users about the benefits and risks of using Bitcoin for international transactions.

The infrastructure and technology required for Bitcoin adoption in remittances and cross-border transactions need further development and improvement. While Bitcoin itself is secure and efficient, ensuring seamless integration with existing financial systems and remittance platforms requires ongoing technological advancements and cooperation between different stakeholders.

Despite the challenges, several initiatives and platforms have emerged to facilitate Bitcoin remittances and cross-border transactions:

Peer-to-peer (P2P) platforms connect individuals looking to send and receive Bitcoin for remittances directly. These platforms often match users based on their needs and offer competitive exchange rates, bypassing traditional banking intermediaries. P2P platforms have gained traction in regions with limited access to formal banking services, offering a decentralized and accessible solution for remittances.

Some specialized companies have emerged that focus on providing Bitcoin remittance services. These companies typically handle the conversion of Bitcoin to local currency on behalf of the sender, ensuring that the recipient receives the funds in their preferred fiat currency. Such companies may offer lower fees and faster processing times compared to traditional remittance services.

Cryptocurrencies that are based on the value of a fiat currency, stablecoins, have gained attention as a potential solution for mitigating Bitcoin's price volatility in remittances. Initiatives like cryptocurrency remittance corridors aim to establish partnerships between cryptocurrency companies and local financial institutions to facilitate seamless and low-cost remittances.

As the global financial landscape evolves, the use of Bitcoin in remittances and cross-border transactions may become a key driver in reshaping the way money moves across borders and increasing financial inclusion for individuals worldwide. With continued innovation and collaboration, Bitcoin's impact on cross-border transactions could revolutionize international finance and pave the way for a more inclusive and efficient global economy.

Bitcoin's role in emerging markets

Bitcoin, the first and most well-known cryptocurrency, has transcended its original vision as a peer-to-peer electronic cash system to become a transformative force in the global financial landscape. While its adoption and acceptance vary across different regions, Bitcoin has shown particular significance in emerging markets. These markets, characterized by rapid economic growth, technological advancements, and expanding populations, present unique opportunities and challenges for cryptocurrencies. In this section, we will explore Bitcoin's role in emerging markets, examining its impact on financial inclusion, economic development, remittances, and the potential challenges and opportunities it presents.

Financial inclusion, the access to affordable and reliable financial services, is a critical component of economic growth and poverty reduction in emerging markets. However, many individuals in these regions remain underserved or excluded from traditional banking systems due to factors such as remote locations, lack of identification, and limited financial infrastructure. Bitcoin's decentralized and borderless nature offers potential solutions to address financial exclusion in these markets.

Bitcoin allows individuals to create and access digital wallets with just an internet connection, enabling them to send, receive, and store value without relying on traditional banking infrastructure. This accessibility empowers unbanked and underbanked populations to participate in the global economy, conduct transactions, and access financial services previously out of reach.

Remittances, or the money sent by migrant workers back to their families in their home countries, is significant in many emerging economies. Traditional remittance channels often involve high fees and delays, reducing the amount received by recipients. Bitcoin's lower transaction costs and faster processing times can provide a more efficient alternative for remittances, allowing more funds to reach their intended recipients and fostering economic development in the receiving countries.

In emerging markets where small-value transactions are common, Bitcoin's ability to facilitate micropayments can be transformative. It allows for cost-effective transactions even for tiny amounts, enabling businesses and service providers to offer affordable services to a broader customer base. Additionally, Bitcoin's programmability allows for the development of innovative financial services and products, such as microloans and insurance, customized to the specific needs of these markets.

Bitcoin's presence in emerging markets has also opened up new investment opportunities and possibilities for economic development.

In regions with limited access to traditional investment opportunities, Bitcoin and other cryptocurrencies provide an alternative asset class for individuals and businesses seeking to diversify their investment portfolios. Bitcoin's potential for price appreciation has attracted investors in emerging markets, who view it as a hedge against inflation and a store of value.

The decentralized nature of Bitcoin allows entrepreneurs in emerging markets to participate in the global digital economy without the need for traditional financial intermediaries. Blockchain technology, which underpins Bitcoin, has sparked a wave of innovation, with startups in these regions exploring applications in supply chain management, identity verification, and beyond.

Bitcoin's censorship resistance and permissionless nature offer a level of economic empowerment to individuals in emerging markets. It allows them to engage in cross-border trade, access financial services, and participate in global commerce without restrictions or intermediaries.

Despite the potential benefits, Bitcoin's adoption in emerging markets is not without challenges and risks. Bitcoin's price volatility can be particularly challenging for individuals and businesses in emerging markets with limited financial resources. While Bitcoin's price appreciation presents opportunities for investors, it also exposes them to significant risks of losses due to sudden price fluctuations.

Regulatory approaches to cryptocurrencies vary widely among emerging market economies. Some countries have embraced cryptocurrencies, while others have imposed restrictions or outright bans. The lack of clear and consistent regulations creates uncertainty for businesses and users, potentially hampering Bitcoin's widespread adoption in these regions.

Bitcoin's usability and accessibility rely on internet connectivity and access to technology. In regions with limited internet penetration or unstable infrastructure, using Bitcoin can be challenging. Additionally, the complexity of cryptocurrency wallets and key management may deter some users from adopting Bitcoin in emerging markets.

The successful acceptance for Bitcoin and cryptocurrencies in emerging markets requires a level of financial literacy and understanding of digital assets. Lack of education about Bitcoin and its use cases can create barriers to entry and hinder its widespread adoption.

Increasing education and awareness about Bitcoin and cryptocurrencies in emerging markets can play a significant role in their adoption and acceptance. Governments, non-profit organizations, and industry players should collaborate to provide accessible and accurate information to the public, enabling them to make informed decisions about utilizing Bitcoin.

Improving internet penetration and technology infrastructure in emerging markets is essential for expanding Bitcoin's usability. Governments and private sector organizations should invest in building robust and reliable digital infrastructure to support the growth of Bitcoin and other cryptocurrencies.

Clear and balanced regulations can provide a conducive environment for the growth of Bitcoin in emerging markets. Governments should strive to strike a balance between consumer protection and fostering innovation, providing a framework that encourages responsible use of cryptocurrencies while protecting users from potential risks.

Integration of Bitcoin with traditional financial services can close the gap between digital and traditional economies. Partnerships between fintech companies and financial institutions can enable the seamless exchange between Bitcoin and fiat currency, promoting financial inclusion and accessibility.

As the global financial landscape evolves, Bitcoin's impact on emerging markets will likely play an increasingly significant role in shaping economic development and financial inclusion. By embracing the opportunities and solving the challenges, emerging markets have the ability to lead the way in harnessing the transformative power of Bitcoin for the benefit of their populations and economies.

CHAPTER IX

The Future of Bitcoin

Scaling solutions and technological developments

Bitcoin, the world's first and most prominent cryptocurrency, has seen exponential growth in adoption and value since its inception. As its popularity increased, so did the demand for more efficient and scalable solutions to address the challenges posed by its growing user base. Scaling, or the ability to handle a larger number of transactions on the Bitcoin network, has been a pressing issue. In this section, we will explore the various scaling solutions and technological developments that have been implemented to enhance Bitcoin's scalability and improve its overall performance.

As Bitcoin gained popularity, it faced the challenge of scalability. The original design of the Bitcoin network, with its block size limit and fixed block time, limited the number of transactions that could be processed per second. This led to increased transaction fees and longer confirmation times during periods of high demand. The need for scaling solutions became evident to ensure that Bitcoin could handle a higher volume of transactions efficiently and remain a viable and accessible payment system.

Segregated Witness, or SegWit, was one of the first major scaling solutions implemented in Bitcoin. Introduced through a soft fork in August 2017, SegWit aimed to increase the block capacity by removing the signature data from the transaction block and storing it separately. This allowed more transaction data to fit within a block, effectively increasing the block size without actually changing the block size limit.

By implementing SegWit, Bitcoin was able to achieve an increase in the number of transactions processed per second and reduce transaction fees. Additionally, SegWit also addressed a vulnerability known as "transaction malleability," which allowed the modification of transaction IDs without altering the transaction's content.

The Lightning Network is another significant scaling solution that operates as a layer-two protocol on top of the Bitcoin blockchain. It was designed to facilitate faster and cheaper transactions by enabling off-chain transactions between parties. By creating a network of payment channels, users can transact directly with one another without the need to broadcast every transaction to the main Bitcoin blockchain.

The Lightning Network has the potential to drastically increase the transaction throughput of Bitcoin and significantly reduce transaction fees. It also allows for near-instantaneous transactions, making it suitable for microtransactions and other use cases where fast confirmation times are essential.

Schnorr Signatures is a cryptographic signature scheme that provides multiple signature verification within a single transaction. It was proposed as a potential scaling solution for Bitcoin to improve efficiency and privacy. By aggregating multiple signatures into one, Schnorr Signatures reduce the overall size of transactions and, in turn, increase the number of transactions that can fit within a block.

The implementation of Schnorr Signatures in Bitcoin could lead to a more efficient use of block space and further reduce transaction fees. Additionally, it enhances privacy by making it harder to distinguish between multiple signatures within a transaction.

Taproot is a proposed soft fork upgrade for Bitcoin that aims to improve privacy, security, and flexibility. It introduces a new signature scheme known as Taproot, which allows for more complex smart contracts while appearing as a regular transaction to external observers. This reduces the blockchain's overall size and increases scalability by enabling the aggregation of multiple smart contracts into a single transaction.

Taproot also enhances privacy by making it difficult to distinguish between different types of transactions, thus providing users with greater fungibility. The upgrade has garnered significant interest from the Bitcoin community and could potentially be one of the most significant technological developments in the Bitcoin network. Schnorr/Taproot is a combination of the Schnorr Signatures and Taproot upgrades. MuSig2 is the proposed implementation of Schnorr-based multi-signature transactions. It allows multiple parties to collaboratively create a single Schnorr signature, reducing the transaction's size while maintaining the security of multi-signature transactions.

Schnorr/Taproot (MuSig2) has the potential to significantly enhance Bitcoin's scalability by reducing the overall size of multi-signature transactions. It also improves privacy and fungibility by enabling more complex smart contracts and making all transactions look like single-party transactions.

In addition to scaling solutions, various technological developments have been proposed and implemented in Bitcoin to enhance its performance, security, and usability.

As mentioned earlier, Segregated Witness was a significant technological development in Bitcoin, not just for its scaling benefits but also for its improvement in security and transaction malleability. By separating signature data from transaction data, SegWit addressed a vulnerability that could be exploited to modify transaction IDs without altering the transaction content.

The introduction of Schnorr Signatures as a potential upgrade in Bitcoin is a significant technological development. Schnorr Signatures improve the efficiency of transactions by reducing their size, which in turn enhances the network's scalability. Moreover, Schnorr Signatures offer better privacy and security compared to the existing ECDSA (Elliptic Curve Digital Signature Algorithm) signatures.

The Taproot upgrade proposes the introduction of a new signature scheme that enhances Bitcoin's privacy and security. By allowing more complex smart contracts to appear as regular transactions, Taproot reduces the blockchain's overall size, leading to improved scalability. Additionally, it enhances privacy by making it harder to distinguish between different types of transactions.

CoinJoin is a privacy-focused technique that allows multiple users to combine their Bitcoin transactions into a single transaction with multiple inputs and outputs. This makes it more challenging to trace individual transactions and improves the privacy and fungibility of Bitcoin.

Scaling solutions and technological developments are critical to ensuring Bitcoin's continued growth and usability as a global decentralized currency. The implementation of Segregated Witness (SegWit) and the Lightning Network has already demonstrated the potential to improve Bitcoin's scalability and reduce transaction fees. Additionally, proposed upgrades such as Schnorr Signatures, Taproot, and Schnorr/Taproot (MuSig2) hold promise in further enhancing Bitcoin's efficiency, privacy, and security.

Potential challenges and opportunities for Bitcoin's future growth

Bitcoin, the pioneering cryptocurrency, has come a long way since its inception in 2009. As the first decentralized digital currency, it has sparked a global revolution in finance, challenging traditional banking systems and opening up new possibilities for financial inclusion and innovation. However, the road ahead is not without challenges. In this section, we will explore the potential challenges and opportunities that lie ahead for Bitcoin's future growth, examining factors such as scalability, regulation, competition, technological advancements, and the role of institutional investors.

One of the most pressing challenges for Bitcoin's future growth is scalability. As the network's popularity has increased, so has the number of transactions being processed, leading to congestion and higher transaction fees during peak periods. Scaling solutions like Segregated Witness (or SegWit) and the Lightning Network have shown promise in addressing these issues, but further improvements will be necessary to accommodate the growing demand for Bitcoin transactions.

The regulatory landscape for cryptocurrencies, including Bitcoin, varies widely across different countries and jurisdictions. Some governments have embraced cryptocurrencies, while others have imposed restrictions or outright bans. This regulatory uncertainty can create challenges for businesses and users, hindering widespread adoption and investment in Bitcoin.

Bitcoin's dominance in the cryptocurrency market has faced increasing competition from alternative cryptocurrencies, known as altcoins. These cryptocurrencies often offer unique features and use cases that differentiate them from Bitcoin. As the market evolves, Bitcoin will need to continually innovate and modify to maintain its position as the leading digital currency.

While Bitcoin's underlying technology, blockchain, is considered secure, it is not immune to potential vulnerabilities and risks. Cyberattacks, code vulnerabilities, and other technical issues could pose threats to the network's stability and security. Continuous research and development are necessary to address these potential risks and maintain the integrity of the Bitcoin network.

Bitcoin's proof-of-work consensus mechanism requires significant computational power, leading to substantial energy consumption. Concerns have been raised about the impact of Bitcoin mining on the environment, particularly as the network grows and attracts more participants. Finding sustainable and energy-efficient alternatives for securing the network will be essential for Bitcoin's future growth.

One of the most significant opportunities for Bitcoin's future growth lies in financial inclusion. In regions with insufficient access to traditional banking services, Bitcoin provides a viable alternative for individuals to participate in the global economy. Its decentralized and borderless nature allows anyone with an internet connection to generate a digital wallet and access financial services, fostering greater financial inclusion worldwide.

The increasing interest and investment from institutional players present a significant opportunity for Bitcoin's future growth. Major companies, asset managers, and hedge funds have started to allocate funds to Bitcoin as a hedge against inflation and a store of value. Institutional adoption can bring greater liquidity, stability, and legitimacy to the cryptocurrency market, further propelling Bitcoin's growth.

The continuous development of new technologies and innovations in the cryptocurrency space offers opportunities for Bitcoin's growth and improvement. Upcoming upgrades such as Taproot, Schnorr Signatures, and Lightning Network improvements can enhance Bitcoin's scalability, privacy, and efficiency, making it more attractive to users and businesses.

Bitcoin has earned the label of "digital gold" and is thought to be a reliable safe-haven investment in difficult economic times. Investors may turn to Bitcoin as a hedge against the dangers associated with traditional financial systems when global financial crises and inflationary pressures arise. Situations like these may boost interest in and use of Bitcoin, hence accelerating its growth in the future.

There is a great chance for Bitcoin's future growth as a result of its widespread acceptance as a payment method and value storage. Both the utility and value of Bitcoin are expected to rise sharply as more establishments accept it as a form of payment and as users grow accustomed to using it in regular transactions.

CONCLUSION

Recap of key points

Throughout this comprehensive exploration of Bitcoin and its various aspects, we have delved into its history, technology, use cases, challenges, and opportunities. This section aims to provide a recap of the key points covered, highlighting the fundamental aspects of Bitcoin that have shaped its significance in the world of finance and technology.

Bitcoin, introduced in 2009 by an anonymous individual or group known as Satoshi Nakamoto, revolutionized the concept of money by being the first decentralized digital currency. Based on blockchain technology, Bitcoin operates without the need for a central authority, relying instead on a network of nodes to confirm and record transactions. The scarcity of Bitcoin, with a fixed supply capped at 21 million coins, has led to its portrayal as digital gold and a hedge against inflation.

Bitcoin's history is marked by its initial obscurity and limited adoption to its exponential growth and recognition as a legitimate financial asset. From its early days as an experiment among a small community of tech enthusiasts to its breakthrough as a viable digital currency, Bitcoin has endured its share of skepticism and challenges. Major milestones, such as the first Bitcoin transaction, the establishment of cryptocurrency exchanges, and the involvement of institutional investors, have shaped its trajectory.

The underlying technology of Bitcoin is blockchain, an immutable and decentralized ledger that keeps all transactions on the network. Bitcoin transactions are added to blocks, which are then linked together chronologically to form the blockchain. Miners are crucial in validating transactions and securing the network through a process called proof-of-work. Through mining, new bitcoins are created and added to circulation as a reward for miners' efforts.

Bitcoin's key characteristics include decentralization, immutability, transparency, and pseudonymity. Additionally, due to its decentralized structure, which prevents any one party from controlling the network, it is immune to censorship and interference by the government. Because transactions stored on the blockchain cannot be changed or removed, they offer a high degree of security and reliability. While transactions are transparent and traceable on the public ledger, users' identities are pseudonymous, allowing for a degree of privacy.

To participate in the Bitcoin network, users need a Bitcoin wallet to store and manage their digital assets. Bitcoin wallets come in different forms, like software wallets, hardware wallets, and mobile wallets. Each type offers different levels of security and convenience. Users are assigned a private key, a unique cryptographic code, to access and authorize transactions on their wallets.

Exchanges that enable users to purchase, sell, and trade bitcoins for fiat money or other cryptocurrencies are one way to obtain bitcoin. Exchanges facilitate the trade process by serving as middlemen between buyers and sellers. Verification processes, such Know Your Customer, or KYC, and Anti-Money Laundering, or AML mandates, are frequently implemented to guarantee adherence to rules and stop illegal activity.

Apart from exchanges, Bitcoin can be obtained through Bitcoin ATMs and peer-to-peer trading platforms. Bitcoin ATMs function similarly to traditional ATMs, allowing users to buy bitcoins using cash or credit cards. Peer-to-peer platforms enable direct transactions between individuals, bypassing intermediaries and offering greater flexibility in trading.

Bitcoin wallets come in various forms, each with its own advantages and security features. Software wallets, like desktop and mobile wallets, offer convenience and easy accessibility. Hardware wallets provide offline storage and enhanced security, making them suitable for long-term storage of bitcoins. Paper wallets, as a form of cold storage, are physical copies of private keys that can be kept offline for added security.

Securing Bitcoin is of utmost importance to protect against potential theft or loss of funds. Best practices include using strong passwords, enabling two-factor authentication, keeping wallets and private keys secure, using hardware wallets for large holdings, and regularly updating software to guard against vulnerabilities.

Bitcoin's investment potential is a subject of considerable debate. Some investors view Bitcoin as a store of value and a hedge against economic uncertainties, akin to digital gold. Others emphasize its volatility and speculative nature, cautioning investors to diversify their portfolios and exercise caution.

Bitcoin's price volatility is a defining characteristic, with frequent and sometimes substantial fluctuations in its value. Various factors contribute to Bitcoin's price movements, including market demand, supply dynamics, macroeconomic events, regulatory developments, and investor sentiment.

Investors can adopt different approaches to investing in Bitcoin, depending on their risk tolerance and investment objectives. Long-term investment strategies involve holding Bitcoin for extended periods, potentially benefiting from price appreciation over time. Short-term trading strategies involve capitalizing on short-term price movements, requiring active monitoring and timing of trades.

The process of creating and putting new bitcoins into circulation, known as mining, also serves to secure the network by verifying and validating transactions. Miners compete to solve challenging mathematical puzzles; newly generated bitcoins and transaction fees are awarded to the first person to discover a workable solution.

Mining requires specialized hardware, known as Application-Specific Integrated Circuits (ASICs), to perform the intensive computational tasks needed to solve the mathematical puzzles. Additionally, miners need mining software to connect their hardware to the Bitcoin network and participate in the mining process.

The Bitcoin halving is an important event that happens approximately every four years, cutting the block reward for miners in half. This process is designed to control the supply of new bitcoins and create scarcity, making Bitcoin a deflationary asset. The halving has historically been followed by price increases due to reduced inflation.

The regulatory landscape for Bitcoin varies greatly across different countries and regions. While some nations have embraced cryptocurrencies and provided clear regulatory frameworks, others have imposed restrictions or outright bans. Regulatory developments can impact Bitcoin's adoption, usage, and investment attractiveness.

The taxation of Bitcoin varies depending on the country's tax laws and regulations. In some jurisdictions, Bitcoin is treated as property, subjecting it to capital gains tax when sold or exchanged. Keeping accurate records of transactions and seeking professional advice are crucial for complying with tax obligations.

Anti-Money Laundering (or AML) and Know Your Customer (or KYC) requirements aim to prevent illicit activities, like terrorist financing and money laundering, in the cryptocurrency space. Exchanges and other service providers often implement AML and KYC measures to comply with regulations and ensure transparency in transactions.

Altcoins, often called alternative cryptocurrencies, are digital assets that have emerged after Bitcoin. They seek to address specific use cases and challenges that Bitcoin may not fully encompass. Altcoins can vary greatly in their technology, governance, and utility, each catering to a particular niche or audience.

Several popular altcoins have gained recognition and adoption for their unique features and use cases. Ethereum, for example, introduced smart contracts and decentralized applications, allowing developers to build a wide range of applications on its blockchain. Other altcoins, such as Litecoin, Ripple, and Cardano, offer distinct advantages and differentiating factors compared to Bitcoin.

Diversifying one's cryptocurrency portfolio involves investing in a variety of digital assets to spread risk and potential rewards. While Bitcoin is often considered the core holding due to its dominant position, diversification into other cryptocurrencies can provide exposure to different markets and technologies.

Bitcoin's use as a payment method has evolved from its early days as an experimental currency to a widely accepted means of exchange. Various merchants, online platforms, and service providers now accept Bitcoin as a form of payment, enhancing its utility and real-world use cases.

Bitcoin's borderless nature and low transaction fees make it an attractive choice for remittances and cross-border transactions. In regions with insufficient access to traditional financial services, Bitcoin provides an efficient and cost-effective alternative for sending and receiving funds across borders.

Bitcoin's impact in emerging markets is profound, offering opportunities for financial inclusion and economic empowerment. Its decentralized and accessible nature enables individuals in these regions to partake in the global economy and access financial services that were previously out of reach.

Bitcoin's future growth is marked by both challenges and opportunities. Scalability, regulatory uncertainty, competition from altcoins, technological risks, and energy consumption are among the key challenges that need to be addressed. On the other hand, financial inclusion, institutional adoption, technological advancements, global financial crises, and mass adoption present significant opportunities for Bitcoin's continued expansion and relevance.

Bitcoin's journey from a mere whitepaper to a global digital asset has been nothing short of extraordinary. Its transformative impact on finance, technology, and economic empowerment continues to shape the future of global financial systems. Understanding its underlying technology, potential use cases, challenges, and opportunities is essential for investors, businesses, policymakers, and individuals to navigate this ever-evolving landscape of digital currency. As the cryptocurrency space evolves, Bitcoin will remain at the forefront, paving the way for a decentralized and inclusive financial future.

Encouragement to explore further and stay informed

The world of cryptocurrencies, led by Bitcoin, has witnessed unprecedented growth and transformation over the past decade. As this dynamic and rapidly evolving landscape continues to transform the future of finance and technology, it is necessary for individuals, businesses, and policymakers to stay informed and explore further into the world of digital assets. This section aims to encourage readers to delve deeper into the realm of cryptocurrencies, understand their potential, and stay informed about the latest developments and opportunities.

Cryptocurrencies, led by Bitcoin, offer a disruptive and decentralized approach to finance that challenges traditional banking systems and opens up new avenues for financial inclusion and innovation. The potential of cryptocurrencies extends far beyond their role as speculative assets, as they pave the way for a future where financial transactions are conducted efficiently, transparently, and securely on decentralized networks. Embracing this potential requires a willingness to explore and understand the underlying technology, the possibilities it presents, and the potential risks it entails.

The foundation of cryptocurrencies is blockchain technology, which is an immutable and decentralized ledger that keeps all transactions transparently on a network of nodes. Understanding blockchain is crucial to grasp the fundamental value proposition of cryptocurrencies, as it enables trustless and safe peer-to-peer transactions without the need for intermediaries. By diving into the mechanics of blockchain, readers can gain insights into its various applications beyond cryptocurrencies, like supply chain management, digital identity verification, and smart contracts.

Bitcoin may have been the first cryptocurrency, but it is now part of a vast and diverse ecosystem of digital assets, each offering unique features and use cases. Exploring beyond Bitcoin introduces readers to altcoins like Ethereum, Ripple, Litecoin, and Cardano, each with its own technological innovations and market niches. Understanding the differences and potential advantages of these altcoins can enable investors to diversify their portfolios and participate in specific blockchain ecosystems.

For millions of unbanked and underbanked individuals worldwide, cryptocurrencies offer a glimmer of hope for financial inclusion and economic empowerment. By providing access to a decentralized financial system, cryptocurrencies can enable individuals in developing regions to participate in the global economy, send remittances with lower fees, and gain access to basic financial services that were previously inaccessible. Exploring this aspect of cryptocurrencies can inspire readers to recognize their transformative potential in uplifting marginalized communities.

Despite their potential, cryptocurrencies are not without challenges and risks. Price volatility, regulatory uncertainties, security concerns, and the potential for fraud and scams are among the issues that require careful consideration. Staying informed about these challenges empowers readers to make informed decisions, exercise caution, and adopt best practices to safeguard their investments and digital assets.

The regulatory landscape for cryptocurrencies varies significantly from one country to another. Some nations have embraced cryptocurrencies, providing clear regulatory frameworks and fostering innovation, while others have taken a more cautious approach or imposed outright bans. Understanding the regulatory environment in one's jurisdiction is crucial to ensure compliance and protect against potential legal risks.

As readers delve deeper into the world of cryptocurrencies, they can become advocates for responsible use and education. By contributing their knowledge and experiences, they can help dispel myths, demystify the technology, and promote a broader comprehension of the benefits and risks of cryptocurrencies. Educating others about the importance of security, privacy, and responsible investment can contribute to a safer and more informed cryptocurrency community.

The cryptocurrency space is characterized by rapid technological advancements and innovations. Keeping abreast of the latest developments, such as scaling solutions, privacy enhancements, and interoperability protocols, can provide readers with insights into emerging opportunities and potential investment prospects.

The involvement of institutional investors and major corporations in the cryptocurrency market is a significant driver of its growth and acceptance. As institutional adoption increases, readers can gain insights into the institutionalization of cryptocurrencies and its implications for mainstream finance.

The cryptocurrency space is dynamic and continuously evolving, making it essential for readers to stay informed through credible sources and expert insights. Seeking information from reputable cryptocurrency analysts, researchers, and industry experts can help readers make informed decisions and navigate the complexities of this ever-changing landscape.

Exploring the world of cryptocurrencies, led by Bitcoin, presents a vast and exciting journey into the future of finance and technology. By understanding the underlying technology, recognizing the diverse landscape of digital assets, and embracing the potential for financial inclusion and innovation, readers can position themselves as informed and empowered participants in the cryptocurrency revolution. Staying vigilant about the challenges and risks, educating others, and monitoring technological advancements and institutional involvement will further enrich the understanding of this transformative field. As the cryptocurrency space continues to evolve, the encouragement to explore further and stay informed becomes a crucial aspect of unlocking its full potential for a decentralized and inclusive financial future.

Final thoughts on the future of Bitcoin

As we reach the end of this comprehensive exploration of Bitcoin, it is clear that the world's first cryptocurrency has come a long way since its humble beginnings in 2009. From a niche experiment among a small group of tech enthusiasts to a global digital asset with a market cap in the trillions, Bitcoin has proven its resilience and staying power. In this final section, we will reflect on the future of Bitcoin and the key factors that will shape its trajectory in the years to come.

One of the most notable developments in recent years is the perception of Bitcoin as a store of value, similar to digital gold. As global financial uncertainties and inflationary pressures persist, more investors are turning to Bitcoin as a hedge against traditional financial systems' risks. This newfound reputation has been further solidified by institutional investors, major corporations, and asset managers allocating significant funds to Bitcoin as part of their investment strategies. As this trend continues, Bitcoin's position as a store of value is likely to strengthen, bolstering its attractiveness as a long-term investment option.

The involvement of institutional investors has been a game-changer for the cryptocurrency market, providing increased liquidity, stability, and legitimacy. As more institutions recognize the potential of Bitcoin and other digital assets, their adoption will likely accelerate. Institutional interest has also prompted the development of more robust custodial solutions, security measures, and regulatory frameworks to cater to the needs of these large-scale investors. This institutionalization of cryptocurrencies has the potential to further drive mainstream adoption and propel Bitcoin into new heights.

The ongoing development of technological advancements and scaling solutions will be crucial in shaping Bitcoin's future. Innovations like the Lightning Network, Schnorr Signatures, Taproot, and Schnorr/Taproot (MuSig2) offer potential solutions to address Bitcoin's scalability challenges and enhance its privacy and efficiency. As these upgrades continue to be implemented, Bitcoin's transaction throughput and usability are expected to improve significantly, making it a more viable option for everyday transactions and micropayments.

One of the pressing concerns surrounding Bitcoin's future growth is its energy consumption. As the mining process requires substantial computational power, the impact of Bitcoin miningon the environment has come under scrutiny. While the industry is exploring energy-efficient alternatives and renewable energy sources, addressing this issue remains a critical aspect of Bitcoin's sustainable future. Balancing energy consumption and network security will be essential to ensure Bitcoin's continued growth while mitigating its ecological footprint.

The regulatory field for cryptocurrencies continues to evolve globally. Some countries have embraced cryptocurrencies, providing clear guidelines and fostering innovation, while others have taken a more cautious approach or imposed restrictions. As the regulatory environment matures, it is essential for policymakers to balance protecting consumers and promoting innovation in the cryptocurrency space. A clear and conducive regulatory framework can provide greater certainty for businesses, investors, and users, fostering a thriving and responsible cryptocurrency ecosystem.

Bitcoin's potential to foster financial inclusion and empowerment remains a driving force behind its continued growth. In regions with insufficient access to traditional financial services, Bitcoin provides an alternative for individuals to participate in the global economy, send remittances, and access basic financial services. As awareness and adoption of cryptocurrencies increase, the impact on financial inclusion and economic empowerment could be transformative, offering millions of people greater control over their financial lives.

Bitcoin's inherent price volatility has been a defining characteristic, attracting both speculators and long-term investors. Navigating this volatility requires a balanced approach, acknowledging the potential for significant short-term fluctuations while focusing on the long-term fundamentals. Additionally, understanding the influence of investor sentiment and market sentiment can provide insights into potential price movements and investment trends.

The success and future of Bitcoin rely heavily on collaboration and community engagement. The decentralized nature of the cryptocurrency space necessitates the collective efforts of developers, businesses, investors, and users to drive innovation, security, and adoption. Contributing to open-source projects, supporting initiatives for financial inclusion, and engaging with the community can foster a more inclusive and vibrant Bitcoin ecosystem.

The future of Bitcoin is characterized by both challenges and opportunities. As a store of value, Bitcoin has established its position as a digital asset with the potential to serve as a hedge against traditional financial risks. The involvement of institutional investors and the ongoing development of technological advancements have the potential to enhance Bitcoin's scalability, efficiency, and security. Addressing environmental concerns and navigating the regulatory landscape are critical considerations for its sustainable growth.

Looking ahead, the transformative potential of Bitcoin to foster financial inclusion and empower individuals globally cannot be underestimated. As we continue to explore the future of Bitcoin, it is essential to stay informed, remain open to technological developments, and embrace responsible and sustainable practices. By doing so, we can collectively contribute to shaping a future where Bitcoin and cryptocurrencies play a pivotal role in creating a more decentralized, inclusive, and resilient global financial system. As we embark on this journey, the future of Bitcoin holds immense promise and potential, driven by the passion and commitment of its diverse and ever- expanding community.

Thank you for buying and reading/ listening to our book. If you found this book useful/ helpful please take a few minutes and leave a review on the platform where you purchased our book. Your feedback matters greatly to us.

9 798869 090560